NEVER A DULL MOMENT

A Memoir

NEVER A DULL MOMENT

A Memoir

SIR PATRICK SHEEHY

In association with:
Alan Ogden

NINE ELMS BOOKS

Nine Elms Books

First published in 2016 by Nine Elms Books Ltd

An independent imprint of Bene Factum Publishing Ltd

Unit 6B
Clapham North Arts Centre
26-32 Voltaire Road
London SW4 6DH

Email: inquiries@bene-factum.co.uk

www.bene-factum.co.uk

ISBN: 978-1-910533-22-2

A CIP catalogue record of this is available from the British Library.

Design and typesetting by Alex Thornton, www.alex22362.com

Printed in the UK

FOREWORD

I have written this memoir primarily in response to the wishes of my children and grandchildren to know more about my life and times, especially since my business career made great demands on the amount of time I could spend at home.

Selling cigarettes around the world is not a particularly noteworthy or honourable occupation other than tobacco raises revenues for governments to spend on other social projects.

But I am immensely proud of having being part of B.A.T., a company of exacting standards, convivial people and great business acumen. We rewarded our shareholders well over the years I worked there and grew the company exponentially at the same time.

I started off my working life as a Second Lieutenant in the Irish Guards. I finished it as a Captain of Industry. None of this could have been achieved without the support and understanding of my ever loving wife.

Patrick Sheehy

December 2015

Chapter One

I hardly knew my parents, John and Jean Sheehy.

My father, John Francis Sheehy, was born in Tuam County in Galway in 1889. His father, a descendant of the Sheehys of Dunquin in County Kerry, was a sergeant in the Royal Irish Constabulary. Brought up in Ireland, my father eventually went to university in Dublin where he studied Classics. In 1913 he passed the Indian Civil Service [ICS] exam in open competition and was posted to Bengal. One of the attractions of the ICS at that time was a pension of £1,000 per annum – it was still that in 1945. He believed that on that sum, he could live like a king in Ireland on his retirement. As it turned out, after the 1922 troubles in Ireland, as a proud British citizen and anti- Sinn Féin, he never returned there. He rarely spoke to me or my sisters about his parents or siblings though he did mention he had a brother, Michael, in the Public Works Department in Burma.

During the 1914-18 War my father joined the Indian Army and saw service in Mesopotamia. After the War he re-joined the ICS and was posted to Burma. Among the positions he held there the most important was warden of the oilfields, where he made lifelong friends with some of the management and with other civil servants in the Finance Department in Rangoon. He was very fond of the Burmese whom he greatly respected and admired. He admired one Burmese lady to such an extent that he fathered a child with her.

Apart from his work which he enjoyed, his recreation was reading the Latin and Greek Classics and playing golf. He was Burma champion and Captain of the Rangoon Golf Club [RGC]. As a scratch golfer he later encouraged me to take up the game; at times it has been an obsession and probably still is! Coincidentally, my wife's father was Captain of the RGC the year my father was champion and vice versa for her father. My father's political inclinations were left of centre. He was a worldly man with no deep religious convictions, even though he was brought up a Catholic.

In 1935 Burma was granted independence from India. Hitherto, the British Government had considered them as one entity. He was offered the choice of leaving the ICS and joining the Burma Civil Service. He chose the greater opportunity of India, so he left his beloved Burma and joined the ICS Finance Department in New Delhi. His last leave in England was in 1935. Then, because of the Second World War, he stayed on in New Delhi without leave, until partition and independence in 1947.

Muhammad Jinnah, Pakistan's first Governor-General, asked him to join the Finance Ministry in Karachi. However my father foresaw the troubles that arose on partition and did not want to be associated with them. He left India, throwing into the sea as he left the pistol he had kept for his self-protection. After a short leave, he took up a post in Germany with the Allied Military Government. He was appointed Assistant Financial Adviser to the Military Governor of the British Zone of West Germany, based in Berlin. For a while he lived there, then in Minden and finally Vlotho, both towns in North Rhine Westphalia.

It was on one of his leaves from Burma that he met and married my mother, Jean Newton Simpson, the daughter of John Archibald Forbes Simpson and Ethel Newton Scott. Both my maternal grandmother and grandfather were born and bred in Scotland. However, when my grandfather joined a firm of jobbers on the London Stock Exchange they settled in Putney, where my mother was born. When they became more prosperous they moved to Orpington and, finally in the 1930s, to Seal near Sevenoaks in Kent.

My Aberdonian grandfather was a caricature of a careful Scot. He was a sparse, ascetic character who looked like a well-groomed Steptoe. He abhorred waste and over-indulgence. A jobber in mining shares on the London Stock Exchange, he worked incessantly and only retired from the City when he was 80. When he was at home, he was in his garden working. I never saw him read a book, indeed I cannot recall there being any books in the house. Apart from gardening, his only recreation was walking, mostly along the road, so that he could time his speed by the mileposts – one mile equalled a quarter of an hour. When you walked with him, you had to keep in step or else you annoyed him. He was a disciplinarian and once told me how walking across London Bridge to Cannon Street one day, two soldiers had ambled past him walking out of step. This incensed him so much that he shouted at them like a drill sergeant "For God's sake, get in step!"

Generally a humourless man, I do recall one joke he told me. Sitting next to Churchill at dinner was Vic Oliver, the Austrian-born comedian who was married to Churchill's daughter Sarah. Oliver asked him who he would like to be if he was not Churchill. He replied "Mussolini". "Why that dreadful Fascist?" exclaimed Oliver to which Churchill retorted "At least he had the guts to shoot his son-in-law".

In contrast, my grandmother was a blowsy lady who enjoyed extravagance – which she called luxury – and was only interested in herself and her two Pekingeses. She completely dominated my grandfather. I stayed with them on and off from 1944 to 1948. She was 90 when she died in the 1960s. They had two children, my mother and my uncle Ian.

I cannot ever remember my mother reminiscing about a happy childhood or adolescence. She did have an adequate education and enjoyed the cosmopolitan life of London. She was fond of musicals and dancing and joined a dancing academy where she met my father. They were married in Burma where my sisters Ann and Mary and I were born. She stayed on with my father when we were sent to boarding school in England. They moved to India in 1935 and stayed there throughout the War in New Delhi. During the War my mother joined the Women's Auxiliary Corps [India] and after working in New Delhi was later transferred to Kandy in Ceylon to join Lord Mountbatten's headquarters of the South East Asia Command, where she was a confidential cypher clerk.

I was born in Rangoon in Burma on 2 September 1930. The Registrar in Rangoon at that time was Maurice Collis, the Irish author of several books about Burma including the striking title 'Lords of the Sunset: A tour of the Shan States'. The first three years of my life were unremarkable. At the age of three, together with my sisters Ann, nearly five, and Mary, twenty-one months, I embarked with our nanny, known as Nurse Hayes, and sailed for England where boarding kindergarten awaited us. 'Woodlands' was so named, not because it was situated in the woods, but because it was run by two spinsters, the Misses Woods. Great Missenden in Buckinghamshire was the nearest town. All the other boys and girls were the children of fathers working in the Far East.

In the 1930s there were no prophylactics to prevent malaria which was debilitating, particularly for children; quinine was the standard treatment. So, in the interest of our health, Woodlands looked after us 365 days of the year. In the summer holidays we all went off to the seaside at Frinton. Apart from these holidays, my only other memory is standing out on the drive one night as the school burned down. Consequently we were relocated to Leighton Buzzard where the school had re-established itself. Surprise is often expressed that I didn't miss my parents or feel lonely. My experience and observation over the years is that parents miss their children far more than children miss their parents. True, in early adulthood one did not have a home life to relate to, but this was balanced by the necessity to stand on one's own two feet. However, with girls I suspect the experience is more of a disadvantage. Home-making is important to them and certainly my sisters resented the lack of a home.

In 1935 my parents came back on leave from Burma. Until the 1939-45 War, tours of duty were four years with six months leave. We were taken out from Woodlands for several daily treats, some with my mother's brother, Uncle Ian, who once arranged a speedboat trip. In 1937 we returned with Nurse Hayes for a six-month visit to India, which involved a four week voyage each way. To avoid annoying other passengers, we were figuratively kept on a very short leash.

My father was now at the Central Board of Revenue in New Delhi and had an impressive office in the Lutyens Building, which we used to visit. Mary and I were disappointed that we were considered too young to go on a trip to Agra to see the Taj Mahal. My father took Ann. I learned a little Hindustani on this trip which I used to the astonishment of my Indian colleagues when I later visited the country on business with British American Tobacco [BAT].

I was at Woodlands in 1939 when we all listened to the wireless and heard the Declaration of War. It was the first political or economic event which registered in my life for I had been completely unaware of 'the slump', unemployment or Neville Chamberlain's 'Peace with Honour'. In mid-September I left Woodlands for Welbury Park preparatory school in Hertfordshire which was run by Mr and Mrs Kenworthy-Browne. I was not happy there. I particularly disliked the corporal punishment which involved lying over the side of the bed with one's trousers down and being given 'six of the best' with a thick leather strap.

A back-breaking and boring task was digging potatoes as a contribution to the war effort. The only other memory of this school was being summoned by Mr Kenworthy-Browne and told I was going to be evacuated to Australia. This was followed by a talk about the dangers I could face from women. I had no idea of the sex act and was more bewildered than wise.

I was nine when my sisters and I boarded the P&O liner 'Stratheden' in Liverpool in August 1940. The ship was still in her peacetime configuration. The cabins and the crew had not been altered for troop ship duties nor had the ship been camouflaged. The passengers were all civilians and it was very comfortable. We joined a convoy of cargo and troop ships off Liverpool and sailed round Northern Ireland and then far out into the Atlantic, because France by now was under occupation and the U-boats were very active. However, there were no incidents involving our convoy and we anchored off Freetown, Sierra Leone, and took on drinking water. The convoy proceeded to Cape Town and up the eastern coast of Africa.

During this part of the voyage the 'Stratheden' left the convoy and headed for Bombay. The troop ships and cargo ships went on up the Red Sea to Suez – no doubt to reinforce the army in North Africa. During the six weeks voyage to Bombay we had the run of the ship – it was great fun. We were spoiled by the crew and not in any way molested, which might be the case today. They did, however, introduce me to smoking cigarettes.

In Bombay we were met by our parents and stayed with them in a flat on Malabar Hill. We were in Bombay for about a week or ten days and then re-embarked on the 'Stratheden' bound for Australia. My mother joined us on the ship to settle us in schools in Australia. The ship called at Colombo, Singapore, Perth, Melbourne and Sydney, where we disembarked. We were put straight into school – my sisters at The Sacred Heart Convent at Rose Bay and me at St Ignatius College, Riverview.

Before my mother went back to India, we had one day out at a restaurant on a pier in Rose Bay. After lunch we hired a rowing boat, but my seamanship skills were found wanting and we had to be rescued. I suspect that by this time my mother had had enough of us. After four or so weeks on a boat, she was anxious to get back to my father in India. Her intention was to return a year later in December 1941 to be with us for Christmas and some of the long Australian 'summer' holidays. In the meantime she had arranged for us to go to a sheep station in north western New South Wales for Christmas 1940.

St Ignatius College, Riverview, is a Jesuit School and one of the Great Public Schools of Australia. There were seven of these schools who had teams in all sports and competed against one another. Sport was most important. The pupils were housed in divisions by age, rather than the English public school system of houses with students of all ages. Discipline was enforced by the division master. Again, unlike the English system, there was no authority invested in any of the boys, so it was very much boys versus masters.

Discipline was enforced by a thick, fairly rigid, black strap which the division master kept in his back pocket concealed by a black-winged cassock or soutane. It was predominantly a boarding school. Most of the boys were from country districts – known as the outback – and were used to a carefree, tough life. The tougher and rougher you were, the better you survived. I started in the lowest division with some seventy other boys. I was the only English boy as evacuation from England to Australia at that time was most unusual. After the fall of Hong Kong, Malaya and Singapore to the Japanese in 1942, we received ten or twelve more evacuees, but in December 1940 I was the only 'Pom'.

The first thing that startled me was the profane vocabulary, not the accent: 'fuck', 'cunt', 'shit' and 'bugger' etc. were freely used expletives. For some time I did not even know what they meant. I was teased and taunted and verbally abused and physically harassed as a 'Pom'. Finally, I confronted one of the ringleaders in a fight. I didn't lose and thereafter I was accepted. Being accepted meant joining in the general mayhem which frequently took place in the dormitory after lights out. We certainly succeeded in irritating our division master, Father Sullivan, who would resort to his strap, usually at random, and I had my fair share. He was particularly adept at hitting the tips of our fingers on a cold morning. Winter in Sydney can be very chilly.

My four years at Riverview were very enjoyable. In winter I played rugby for one of their many XVs and in summer enjoyed swimming and coxing the fours and eights of the older boys. In my last year I coxed for the school eight in two regattas. In one of them, the Riverview regatta, we were rowing to the start when the rowlock of our stroke came off. We made hasty repairs but unfortunately these did not work and we only completed 200 yards of the course. In the other regatta, on the Parramatta River, eight 'Eights' were in the middle of the river being watched by boys aboard ferries hired by all the schools involved. On the way to the start, I steered our eight past the Riverview ferry. We were loudly cheered, which I proudly acknowledged, until 'boom!' we crashed into a motorboat crossing our bow. Fortunately, the only damage was to the tip of our bow and we came in a respectable fourth.

I do not recollect learning very much at Riverview. There were about thirty-five to forty boys per class and, apart from the occasional letter from my father expressing disappointment at my lack of progress, nobody took any special interest. There was one absurd subject – elocution – taught at the school by a visiting Englishman, Mr Harry Thomas. His aim was to get us to speak 'Oxford English'. The classes were a riot. Mr Thomas would ask us to repeat after him: 'Mr Brown went to town to buy a brown dressing gown which cost one pound' and, even more comically: 'Brown's cow's manure'. Rolls of toilet paper aimed at Mr Thomas would come whizzing through the window. Needless to say, after four years I was fluent in 'strine'.

Every two or three weeks we had a free weekend and most boys visited relatives in and around Sydney. I used to get permission to go and see my sisters at their Convent in Rose Bay. This entailed getting the ferry to Circular Quay in the centre of Sydney and then taking a tram to Rose Bay. While I was happy to see my sisters, the real purpose of my visit was to get hold of their surplus pocket money. During the term, if they left Rose Bay at all, it was with another girl and her parents. To enter that Convent with its awesome nuns and giggling girls was a daunting experience for a 10 or 11-year-old boy. Many a time after getting off the tram, I walked up and down the road outside the Convent for up to an hour, plucking up the courage to enter.

Holidays were the greatest fun. Before our mother left us in November 1940, she had arranged for the three of us to spend the 1940 Christmas holiday with the McKay family at their sheep station called The Overflow. It was a barefoot and bareback riding life which I thoroughly enjoyed. Towards the end of the holiday they rented a house at Cronulla, a surfside resort near Sydney. Bert was the father, Florence the mother, John the eldest son and Susan, Jane and Michael his siblings. A genial typical sheep station owner with a broad rim hat and open shirt, Bert was sadly dying from cancer. I remember I went to visit him one afternoon in hospital. Florence became very much a surrogate mother to me when I was in Australia. After the War, she came over to England a couple of times; much to my delight she attended my daughter's wedding.

Apart from going back to The Overflow two or three times in the years that followed, sometimes with my sisters, I spent the remainder of the holidays with other evacuee boys. By the spring of 1942 the Japanese progress through Asia led to expatriate children from all over South East Asia being shipped to Australia. The closest I got to the war was a visit to the two Japanese midget submarine that were on show, having been sunk after penetrating the defences of Sydney harbour in June 1942.

At Riverview there was some eight to ten of us in the same boat as it were. Summer holidays I recall were spent as a group at Seven Mile Beach, the 'Blue Mountains', Penrith and Lake Macquarie, where we lodged with the superintendent of the largest mental hospital in New South Wales. The manager of the hotel or boarding house accepted responsibility for us, but I do not recall ever being reprimanded. We did what we liked.

My father used to send me aerograms every month or so. Apart from telling me he had been awarded a Knighthood in 1943, most of his letters expressed disappointment at my exam results and poor school reports. Indeed, I had fallen to thirty-third in a class of thirty-five. I had also written to my father that I wanted to be a sheep farmer. He was clearly having none of that!

Chapter Two

In 1944, out of the blue, letters arrived from my father to me and the head-master saying that he had arranged for me to be shipped back to England and to go to Ampleforth. I was desolate. I was having a marvellous time, both at school and in the holidays. I had fondly imagined that I would become a 'Jackaroo' on leaving Riverview or go to agricultural college and that my father would buy me a sheep station. Of course I did not realise how little the ICS paid, but I knew he was a Knight and assumed he was wealthy. All these dreams were now shattered. The prospect of returning to school in England where I had been unhappy added to my gloom and misery, for I clearly remember being very distressed. I stood on the deck of the ship on the voyage from Sydney to Melbourne and cried and cried. For the first time I felt lonely and unloved.

I joined a British India Steam Navigation cargo-cum- passenger boat – a 'BI ship' – which called at Melbourne, where we were delayed for a week or so on account of a dock strike. Despite the War and the fact that our cargo boat included supplies for troops in Burma, the dockers were more interested in their pay. We eventually proceeded on to Freemantle from where we sailed for Colombo. The ship made this voyage on its own and not in convoy, despite the fact that the Indian Ocean was infested with Japanese submarines. Small warships suitable for escort did not have the range and the larger ones were required for more offensive action.

The passengers included a number of women and children, as well as us men. Curiously, the women and children were accommodated in the lower decks or bowels of the ship, whilst the men enjoyed the first class cabins on the boat deck. The thinking seemed to be that were the ship to be torpedoed, women and children would be tiresome in the lifeboats, so it was preferable they went down with the ship. Even though I was only 13, being included in the men's category, I enjoyed the luxury of the first class cabins. In return for this privilege, we had to do submarine watch throughout the night, scouring the seas for any signs of enemy submarines.

We arrived at Colombo without incident. My mother, who was working at Supreme Headquarters South East Asia Command at Kandy at the time, met me and we went to stay at The Galle Face Hotel. It was teeming with Admirals, Air Marshals, Generals and Brigadiers. My mother was horrified by and somewhat ashamed of my Australian accent, especially when I was introduced to her top brass friends and replied "pleased to meet you." She then had to return to Kandy while I waited for another ship to take me to England.

First of all I was billeted at a manse with a Church of Scotland Minister. When I had outstayed my welcome there I spent a week or two with a British American Tobacco [BAT] representative, John Hill. It was rather dreary. The next ship eventually arrived from Calcutta. It was totally different to the BI ship, somewhat smaller and basically a cargo ship, with very limited passenger accommodation and no first class cabins. The two berth cabins had been converted to six berths, so it was impossible for more than one person to wash or dress at a time. The cargo was jute and bound for Dundee.

I had never shared a cabin with adults before and at 14 it was an instructive experience, though I was never molested. Apart from myself, there was a chartered engineer from Tata, a scrawny bearded Englishman. In a lower bunk was a tea planter from Assam, a large fleshy man who spent most of the voyage in it. He liked to reminisce with me about life on his plantation and in particular how he used to ask the field supervisor to provide him with a female tea picker for his evening pleasure. To this end he had an ample supply of condoms, one of which he showed me. He told me he'd had enough of India. Along from the tea planter, the occupant of the next bunk was a ship's Captain who claimed that his ship had been sunk. Maybe that was the cause of his heavy drinking. He started on the gin as soon as the bar was open. He slept most afternoons, but resumed with whisky in the evenings. Most nights he and the chartered engineer kept us awake with bawdy songs. In the bunk above the ship's captain was a dapper, quiet man who was politeness itself and kept himself to himself. On the opposite side of the cabin I had the top bunk.

Below me was a Quaker. I think he was from St John's Ambulance Service. He had the zeal of a missionary and appeared to find our company distasteful. For some reason I must have got on his nerves. One day, he cornered me on the boat deck intending to wallop me. We exchanged punches and, as far as I was concerned, the outcome was a draw. For the rest of the voyage we had little to say to one another.

Between Colombo and Aden our ship sailed alone. One afternoon a raft with a tattered sail was sighted. There were some bodies with limbs poking out from under the canvas. We circled, hooting noisily, to see if anyone stirred. Finally we gently nudged the raft but did not stop as such a situation was often a decoy for a Japanese submarine. Otherwise, the trip was uneventful until we reached Southampton. Food had been monotonous, with 'bubble and squeak' for lunch and again for dinner, day in and day out.

At Southampton we took on some fresh vegetables for the two day dash up 'E-Boat alley' to Dundee. We docked at Dundee on a cold but crisp November morning. There were dockers to unload the cargo of jute, but not to unload the passengers' baggage. I recall spending the whole morning humping suitcases and trunks for fellow passengers from the ship to the train. We travelled overnight to King's Cross. Shortly after getting off the train, I heard the sound of a V2 rocket exploding – a distant thud, followed some seconds later by several reverberations. The people around me appeared unconcerned, just getting on with what they were doing. I heard one or two more V2s while I was in London that day. I got a taxi to Charing Cross and caught the train to Tub's Hill, the station for Sevenoaks. Here I was met by Granny Ethel who drove me to her house, Fir Trees, in Seal, where I was to stay until I went to Ampleforth in January.

If a secret of marriage is for a husband and wife to have contrasting personalities, this was certainly true of Granny and Grandpa Simpson. Granny Simpson was a large, plump woman with a sallow complexion. A staunch Conservative, she had a pleasant but commanding manner. Her friend, a former Lord Mayor of London, used to call her 'The Duchess' because of her name and her personality. She was obsessed with her health, particularly what she believed was a weak heart. She would only go upstairs and downstairs once a day. She was convinced she would have a heart attack at night – so much so that Grandpa Simpson, in the latter years, used to sleep on a mattress on the floor at the end of her bed.

Granny loved what she called 'luxury'. Before the War, without her husband who remained at work, she enjoyed going on luxury cruises and then during the War she frequented luxury hotels in north Wales, Scotland and Eastbourne. Their son Ian and daughter-in-law Lizzie were both in the Army, but managed to get leave at the same time. Lizzie was a tall, pretty, blonde Dane who had come over to England at the start of the War and enlisted as a staff car driver. Her staff officer passenger turned out to be Uncle Ian who had been a Captain in the Honourable Artillery Company before the War. He was a delightful man with a legion of friends, but somehow never managed to make a success of anything. He must have been one of the very few officers to have started off as a captain in 1939 and ended as one in 1945.

Warmly welcomed at first into this household, I was kept away from the neighbours because of my Australian accent. After a few weeks the welcome wore off and I was just tolerated. The feeling was mutual. After a while I was threatened that if I did not behave in a more conciliatory and polite manner, I should be banished to living in the pub in the village. Unfortunately the threat was never carried out.

As to what I did all day, I remember very little. Occasionally we would have to take the potato peelings and other food waste to the pig club for those who provided food for the pigs were entitled to portions of pork over and above their meat rations. One day we walked a mile or so up the road to see a demolished house that had been hit by a V2. Once or twice the siren sounded for a doodlebug, but fortunately they flew over. Long convoys of military vehicles used to rumble along the road at the end of the garden on their way to the coast.

I slept in my grandfather's room on a bed at the end of his bed. I was allowed a bath twice a week, but with only 4 inches of hot water. Grandpa instinctively knew when anyone had had their 4 inches. He would bang on the door and order the tap to be turned off. Granny was in charge of rationing out the food. It seemed to me that she always ended up with the larger portions.

I do not recall the neighbours or villagers being anything other than cheerful and polite. All seem to have stayed put throughout the War. Some were worried for their children who were POWs. Few houses had air raid shelters. Alarms were part of life's routine. Apart from the rationing, life in the English countryside was pretty normal.

In January 1945 I went off to Ampleforth after nearly three months at Fir Trees. I was looking forward to the boarding school way of life with which I was very familiar. I do not recall my grandmother expressing any regret on my departure. There was a school train from King's Cross to York. One of the games on the train was to insert the head of a match into the hollow of a key and, with another lighted match or cigarette, heat the handle end of the key barrel until a flaming match flew out of the end of it. Little did I know that on a previous Ampleforth school train some boys had started a fire with calamitous consequences.

It was a long, corridor-less carriage, so supervision of the boys was minimal. The train trundled along to York, taking at least four hours. The school carriages were then uncoupled and attached to another engine and we puffed along even more slowly to Gilling East, where we detrained onto buses for the school.

Ampleforth was different from St Ignatius College in Sydney, which had been divided into divisions by ages. It had houses comprising boys of all ages and I was put into St Bede's. The housemaster was a Father Paulinus Massey, familiarly known as 'Pinky'. He was a nice man, neither a scholar nor a sportsman. He let the monitors and prefects run the house. In Australia the division master was responsible for discipline. Here, out of the classroom, it was the monitors.

If you misbehaved in the classroom at Ampleforth, you got extra work periods or, for persistent misbehaviour, you were sent to the housemaster who beat you with a strap on the hand. Monitors could punish you by giving you any number of lines or time on The Walk, which was a stretch of road about fifty yards long, which you had to walk up and down in silence with your hands out of your pockets for a prescribed time.

I was astonished at the good behaviour of the boys at Ampleforth, compared to the frequently riotous state of my division house in Australia. The calm was almost boring. Another remarkable contrast was the boys' vocabulary. The foul language which was so prevalent in Australia was never heard at Ampleforth. My Australian accent was a source of constant teasing, but I had already survived far worse teasing four years earlier for being a 'Pom'.

Initially placed in Lower 4B, the second lowest class in the school, by the end of the summer term I had progressed to Middle 5B. There was a house cricket and swimming team for sports. I didn't take to another option, beagling. We were kept fully occupied and there was little time off except Wednesdays which were half days. There were no half terms, no weekend exeats and hardly any parental visits. Petrol was severely rationed and certainly not used for taking boys to and from school.

We followed the War quite closely and joined in the rejoicing at the Allied victory over the Germans. VE Day was celebrated with two days holiday. These were spent at Ampleforth. On one of them, a few of us went over to the lakes on the other side of the valley. We found a derelict boat and paddled out it into the middle of a lake where it began to sink. Fully clothed we abandoned ship. Unfortunately a boy called Swarbrick couldn't swim and after a struggle with me, during which I thought I was going to drown, we pushed the half-sunken boat towards him and he managed to cling on to it and save himself.

My parents were still in India and my sisters in Australia. For the summer holidays I was billeted with a Major General and his wife in Essex. It was an uneventful six weeks. In September I moved into the middle fifth form, so I must have done quite well in my first two terms. It was in the fifth form that you studied for the School Certificate and matriculation. I couldn't get on with Latin, Greek and Algebra though I enjoyed French and History. Most of all I enjoyed rugby and was selected for the school's Colts side. I was, I remember, becoming aware of the menace of Soviet Communism, lying awake at night worrying about Britain being overwhelmed and suffering all the horrors of Soviet labour camps, torture and massacres which one read about.

In 1946 my mother and my sisters returned to England. My sisters came from Australia round The Cape. My mother returned in anticipation of India's independence. They set up home in a flat in Gledhow Gardens in Kensington. At this time, my father was still flying to and from India on Government affairs. He did once come to visit me at Ampleforth. It was the only time in 15 years at boarding school that I remember him visiting me. Ann, my eldest sister, went to Bedford College for Women at London University in Regent's Park. Mary went to The Convent of the Sacred Heart at Tunbridge Wells.

That summer I duly took the School Certificate aged 15 and achieved matriculation, and thereby was promoted, in September, to the sixth form, where one prepared for the Higher School Certificate. That summer my mother, my sisters and I went to St Brelade's Bay in Jersey for six weeks. The island and the islanders seemed to have survived the War pretty well. I remember being asked whether the islanders wore gold trunks in the swimming gala featuring races between the islanders and the mainlanders. I bicycled all around the island and wherever possible I bought postcards of the coastline, which I still have somewhere.

The 1946 and 1947 school years were pretty uneventful. In the sixth form I concentrated on French and History as my main subjects. Subsidiary subjects were Latin, Politics and Economics. Through Politics and Economics I began to understand my father's socialist leanings. At this time the majority of the boys and teaching monks were Tories. I inclined to follow my father.

I was appointed a house monitor and selected for the First XV and the school swimming team. In the summer I passed the Higher School Certificate without distinction. This was certainly not good enough to earn a place at a good Oxford college, which was my ambition.

In the summer holidays of 1947 I took part in the Ampleforth Harvest Camp near Oxford. The work was monotonous, stacking wheat and barley into stooks for there were no combine harvesters around. It was a hot summer and in the evenings we had fun at the nearby pub. From there I went to Brittany with my family and one afternoon near Lannion I was on hand when a woman and a child capsized their canoe and were thought to be drowning. I rushed into the sea to help, but unfortunately hadn't done up my swimming trunks, which slipped to my knees. With one hand on my trunks and the other swimming, I reached her still squawking, but clinging to the upturned canoe. The child in contrast was completely calm.

Shortly after, a boat arrived and as I heaved her up from below, an enormous mound of blubber appeared from beneath the sea and flopped into the boat. Safely ashore and with paddle in hand, with a small crowd behind her, she marched along the beach past the ranks of onlookers, quite the heroine of the piece. Later on we went to Menton. This was not a happy holiday; beach life was dull and there was no fun to be had when short of funds in the South of France.

In the 1947/48 school year I was appointed a monitor, head of my house and captain of rugby and swimming. The scholastic aim was to get a better Higher School Certificate, preferably a scholarship. As I had an ambition to work abroad where life seemed much more exciting than in England, I wasn't particularly fussed whether I went to university or not as I thought the chances of getting a scholarship were not good.

The various roles I had at the school were a distraction from the classroom. I enjoyed most of the responsibilities and the sporting challenges, although one of my responsibilities made me very nervous and uncomfortable. One of the monks had found two boys snogging with the maids under one of the buildings. This was seen as an outrageous offence and had to be dealt with by exemplary punishment – a school beating by me, the head monitor. It was a very formal affair with all the monitors present. The culprits came in, one at a time, in their pyjamas and had to stand on the rungs of the chair, and then bend over the back of the chair and grab the front of the seat. The caned six blows were applied to the posterior. The boys who received the beatings were very stoic. It was not an experience that I would ever want to repeat. Ever since, I have abhorred corporal punishment and fully support its eradication throughout the world. Unfortunately, it is still prevalent in Asia and the Middle East.

The headmaster, Paul Neville, known as 'Posh', urged me to go to Christ Church, Oxford. I went there for an interview in the summer of 1948 but failed. About that time Neville also said he had been asked by the Lieutenant Colonel of the Grenadier Guards to nominate one or two boys for the Regiment's places in the Brigade Squad. With my Irish name the Grenadiers did not seem the appropriate regiment, so the opportunity passed anyway and I decided to stay on at school until December.

That summer's holiday started with the school pilgrimage to Lourdes. The party of fifteen Fifth and Sixth formers was led by Father Jerome Lambert. Our transport was the village bus, driven by the aged and agnostic Mr Appleby, proprietor of the Ampleforth Garage. It was an old bus, with a door front and back and a ladder at the rear leading to a large roof rack which stored our luggage. We trundled through France at about thirty miles per hour and, when it was hot, which it frequently was, we took turns to climb onto the roof rack and lounge about on the luggage. Appleby took to wearing the traditional English sun hat, a handkerchief with knots tied in each corner. At night we were billeted at Catholic schools.

At Lourdes we camped. The town was very crowded and outside the sanctuary the souvenir shops were very oppressive. Inside the sanctuary, the aura of holiness was remarkable. We bathed in the waters of the spring but it was more like a quick dip in and out, as it was extremely cold. In the evening we did work as Brancardiers, helping the sick to participate in the candlelit procession. It was a humbling yet inspiring experience. Having travelled down the west coast to Lourdes, we returned via Carcassonne and the centre of France to Paris and back to Calais.

Two other memories of that pilgrimage were of the outrageous flirting of Father Jerome with the waitresses and the quality of the Vermouth that I drank in quantity. When I got back to England I had the most unpleasant stomach pains. The rest of that summer I spent in Minden in Germany with my parents and sisters. It was the first holiday we had spent together since New Delhi in 1937. The journey from Harwich to the Hook of Holland was memorable for the crowds of triumphant Dutchmen celebrating the achievements of Fanny Blankers-Koen who had won the most gold medals of any athlete at the 1948 Summer Games. From the Hook, I took a train which passed through the Ruhr: I can vividly remember the devastation caused by Allied bombing and of the ghost-like figures who emerged from the cellars and stood by the tracks begging for food and cigarettes.

Chapter Three

I returned to Ampleforth that September with the intention of gaining a scholarship to Wadham College, Oxford but I was still head monitor and captain of rugby, which didn't help my studies. In truth, I was not academic material and I duly failed. That term the Irish Guards offered me a place in the Brigade Squad which was due to start in January 1949. On 1 January 1949 the National Service Act was due to come into force, replacing the Emergency Powers Act which had dealt with conscription during the War. Under the new Act, the period of active service was reduced from two years to 18 months but conscripts were required to serve a further two years in the Territorials. As I wanted to work abroad, I did not wish to be tied to this Territorial obligation. The Irish Guards' regimental HQ considerately arranged for me to be conscripted under The Emergency Powers Act.

So, a week after leaving Ampleforth, I joined the Irish Guards at Birdcage Walk and was sent on leave, with full pay, until the middle of January 1949. Christmas was spent at Vlotho where my parents had moved to that autumn. The time soon came to present myself to The Guards Depot at Caterham Barracks. The buildings were of dirty grey brick, sparsely furnished and sparsely heated. The washing facilities were outside. There were a number of parade grounds for drilling. The overall impression was bleak. The barracks were overlooked by a neighbouring lunatic asylum, which looked even more depressing. It was here that the Guards moulded their recruits. The Brigade Squad was made up of potential officers. All of us were from public schools – the majority being from Eton, Harrow and Winchester.

On the face of it, this was a privileged group. While Ampleforth had one or two aristocrats, the Brigade Squad was teeming with them. I was amazed by two or three of them confidently predicting that, after Oxbridge, they would be taking 'the family seat' in the House of Commons. However, for the time being the reality was rather different, for the trained soldiers and sergeants had been instructed to humble us so much that other non-Brigade Squad recruits would be glad they were not in line to be officers.

Punctuated with fatuous exercises, life at Caterham and later at Pirbright was an intellectually undemanding routine, sleeping out in the foxholes in the drizzle, pretending the enemy was in the nearby woods and so on. The prospect of seeing action seemed remote. One incident I recall took place during a war games exercise. The brigadier referee spotted a patrol walking across a bridge and, through his assistant, wanted to know from its leader why they were doing so when there was a sign clearly stating 'Bridge blown'. Back came the explanation: "With respect, Sir, you can't see the notices on our backs – we're swimming."

Mostly life at Pirbright was all about "drill, drill, drill, run, run, run" and when we did have any free time it was "polish, polish, polish" - not only our own kit, but the barracks as well. In a way it was degrading, but in another sense it was uplifting. One was transformed from a scruffy schoolboy into a proud guardsman. My grandfather was delighted at the change he saw in me.

After about six weeks we went off to a War Office Selection Board at Lingfield. This lasted three days, where we were given indoor and outdoor tasks to assess our officer potential. Few failed, but some of my group who passed failed to get an offer of a commission in their chosen regiment. After all the humiliations of the Brigade Squad, this was a bitter disappointment.

My next move was to Officer Cadet School at Eaton Hall, near Chester. This was a huge old pile, formerly the Duke of Westminster's home. I was made an Under Officer and continued my sporting career, swimming for Northern Command in the National Championships at Southport. One disagreeable memory was disgusting behaviour of some Old Harrovians in my platoon who were overtly homosexual.

In May 1949, while at Eaton Hall, I received the shocking news that my father had been murdered at our home in Germany. I joined my sisters in London and we travelled together to Minden where we met my mother. She had accompanied my father when he joined the Control Commission in Germany in 1947 and was with him in the house on the night of the murder. Clearly shocked by the experience, she had recovered her composure by the time we arrived for the funeral. Although I had read about the murder in the papers, my mother filled me in with the details. In the early hours of the morning they had been woken by an intruder who had ransacked the downstairs of the house and had found nothing valuable. My father confronted him on the stairs with a slipper in his hand. The burglar wanted the ring on his finger, which my father refused to give him. He hit him with the slipper. The burglar shot him at point blank range and fled.

The culprit, a German citizen and displaced person who had lost his home when the borders were redrawn at the end of the War, was quickly caught and tried for murder in a Control Commission court. He was convicted and sentenced to death. My mother received appeals from him and his family for this to be reduced to a life sentence. She asked me for my view. I funked giving a straight answer by saying she should leave it for the authorities to decide. Ever since I have regretted not recommending to my mother that she intervene to get the death sentence commuted for I am against capital punishment. Fortunately, the authorities commuted the death sentence to life imprisonment.

Father was duly buried in a military cemetery outside Hanover. When the funeral was over, we all returned to England. My mother had been promised by my grandparents that they would let her have their house in Frinton in Essex. This promise had been made pre-War and was conveniently forgotten when she became a widow with nearly grown-up children. Instead they urged and expected her to go and live at Seal to look after them in their old age. Instead she set up home in a flat in London.

These were hard times for my mother for she had to provide for my sisters who were still at university. Although she had an ICS and Foreign Office pension, she could not get hold of my father's capital as his will had gone missing when his baggage was stolen while he was travelling in Germany. The copy with the Registrar in Rangoon could not be traced.

Until the early 1970s my mother lived in various apartments in parts of South West London. She then moved to Lymington in Hampshire, where she changed house every two or three years or so before finally settling in Sandwich in Kent. She liked playing bridge, fairly viciously. She went on cruises most years and had a contented last twenty years. She died in hospital shortly after surgery.

In spite of the brevity of my acquaintance with my father, I held a deep respect and affection for him. The last time I wept uncontrollable tears of sadness was on hearing of his death. He had had a profound influence on my life. First and foremost, though not a practising Catholic, he sent me to Catholic schools. I am a Catholic. Second, when he got alarmed at my descent to the bottom quartile of my Australian school, he arranged for me to be shipped back to the

UK in 1944, a voyage not without its hazards. But my father believed 'better dead than ill-read'. Had I stayed in Australia, as my sister did, I would probably have lived my life there for what I particularly aspired to was sheep farming. Third, he made it quite clear that if I could not gain a scholarship, he would not subsidise a university education. Thus, I did not go to university. Furthermore he made it quite clear that we could not expect any money from him after the conclusion of our first-class education, which he said had cost him a fortune to provide. We would have to get by on our own. Fourth, he urged me not to join the Civil Service, but to go into business where, compared to the abysmal pay of the Civil Service, there was a good chance to make some money, not difficult as many of the well-off businessmen he knew were bloody fools.

After his death, my relationship with my mother developed into a lasting friendship. I recall little of my early years with her, as from the age of five until I was 17 she never really looked after me and during that time I never visited home, wherever that was. Consequently I never felt dependent on her and thus my relationship with her could best be described as independent. However it was also a relationship of equals and of much affection because she was my most supportive fan and I in turn enjoyed being with her. She never married again and remained fiercely independent until her death. Being of Scottish descent, thrift was one of her virtues; any sense of thrift that I have I owe to her.

I resumed training at Eaton Hall and in the summer of 1949 I was commissioned as an Ensign [Second Lieutenant] in the Irish Guards and posted to the First Battalion at Chelsea Barracks. I was very proud to be a guardsman and even prouder when I first put on my officer's uniform. Pride indeed comes before a fall, because it was soon clear that among the officers, Ensigns were the lowest form of life and, once again, it was very humbling.

In 1949 the regiment had returned from a long and difficult spell in Palestine where they were trying to keep the peace between the indigenous Palestinians and the Jewish settlers who were seeking an independent state. Surprisingly, there was very little discussion about this political problem. If there were any political discussion, it was about the cuts in defence expenditure, where we were only allowed to use our transport on a very limited basis. When I talked to those of my men who had fought in the war, I was struck by how they always reminisced about what happened when they weren't fighting; they never discussed the battles.

The battalion having been overseas for so long, all the officers and men had accumulated extensive leave. So most of the time, it was at a third of its normal strength. We shared Chelsea Barracks with the Third Battalion of the Grenadier Guards and then with the Welsh Guards when they moved to Wellington Barracks. The primary task with the Brigade of Guards in London was public duties, i.e. mounting guard at Buckingham Palace, St James's Palace, The Tower of London, Clarence House, Marlborough House and the Bank of England. As a last resort, we were also there to uphold law and order.

The main event of the calendar was the King's Birthday Parade which was preceded by Spring Drills. As far as the Adjutant, Major Will Berridge, was concerned, I was quite the scruffiest officer in the battalion and, on more than one occasion, he ordered me off the parade ground to get myself smartened up. Perhaps because of this, I never did more than one Buck House guard, which other than the Birthday Parade was the only occasion for appearing in the tunic and bearskin. I did my stints of forty-eight hour guards at the Tower of London or overnight at the Bank of England in khaki battledress.

The Tower guard was particularly tedious. The officer in charge was housed in the officers' mess at the Royal Fusiliers' HQ. The HQ officers did not live in the mess and so one was confined to the large, gloomy building, all alone day and night. The main feature of the two days at the Tower was the Ceremony of the Keys, which took place near The Jewel Tower at ten p.m, when a small select crowd would be invited.

I have two main memories of those boring days. One morning the Chief Yeoman of the Guard complained to me that he suspected that a Guardsman had used his bayonet to prize the lock off the ladies' loo and had stolen the pennies. We paraded the guard and found evidence of bronzing on one guardsman's bayonet. He had stolen thirty pence. A Guardsman's pay in those days was about thirty shillings a day and, what with stoppages, was much less. He was marched off by the Military Police.

Another memory was being awoken one night in the Officer of the Guard's room in the battlements on the Tower Bridge side. As it was hot, I was sleeping with the window open when I was awoken by a ghostly howling noise. It turned out to be several Tower cats singing to the moon.

The other main duty, the Bank of England picket, was more agreeable, but could be hazardous. Presumably to show the citizens of London that the Bank was important, a Guards platoon marched each day from Chelsea Barracks to Threadneedle Street. It was hazardous because you were not allowed to stop in traffic jams or at traffic lights. Officers could become detached from the rest of the platoon, as the noise of vehicles muffled the sound of the tramping of their feet. This was somewhat mitigated in the case of both the Irish and Scots Guards by the sound of a piper marching ahead of the officer. Another reason it was hazardous was because serving and former officers were on hand in the City streets to report any slackness they spotted to the Adjutant. This could result in extra picket duty – a twenty-four hour stint on duty in the barracks - or being confined to barracks.

When you arrived at the Bank for duty, you were welcomed by a pink-coated flunky and shown to the officer's flat. After the Officers' Mess at Chelsea and the extremely Spartan room at the Tower, it was what my grandmother would have described as luxurious. Carpeted throughout, the flat had a sitting room with armchairs, a dining room, kitchen and a bedroom with an ample, comfortable bed and, of course, an en-suite bathroom. Officers were allowed two guests for dinner – but men only. Hence, the vulgar term, the 'wank' picket.

The Bank provided drinks before a fine dinner with claret and port to follow. On duty the picket guard was stationed in various corridors which, in turn, were patrolled by the Bank's security personnel – presumably there to see that the guards did not help themselves to the petty cash. There was another tradition concerning the Bank picket. If it rained on the march, the officer in charge had the discretion to order the guard to continue marching or to go on by Tube, while the officer took a taxi. But the fares for both the Tube and taxi went on his account.

For those not on guard there was little to do at the barracks. Company orders were at ten a.m. I was in No.1 Company, commanded by Major David O'Cock. He lived out of London, so this timing suited him. Second in command was Jim Chichester-Clarke, later to become Prime Minister of Northern Ireland. Jim was a large man, quietly spoken with a gentle personality – the last person you would have thought would become a prominent politician in that troubled province. Sometimes you had to attend battalion orders at noon, but often one was free until the next morning. Occasionally, there were sports afternoons and I played rugby for the Irish Guards in the Household Brigade competitions.

Ensigns had to wear uniform around the barracks but, for officers of the rank of major and above, it appeared to be optional. I seldom saw the Commanding Officer, Lieutenant-Colonel Michael Gordon-Watson, in uniform. There was a strictly enforced civilian dress code for officers: a dark suit with a stiff white collar shirt, highly polished black shoes, black bowler hat and rolled umbrella. In the country or at the races, it was permissible to be seen in a tweed suit with a soft, felt brown hat. If not properly dressed outside the barracks, one would be admonished by the adjutant. The Officers' Mess was very crowded and I shared a room with Pat and Micky Bowen, both of whom had been at Downside. Micky went on to become Archbishop of Southwark.

To ease overcrowding, officers were encouraged by generous allowances to live out of barracks. After six weeks I moved to my mother's flat in Cranleigh Gardens, Kensington. My soldier servant (a 'batman' in other regiments) used to come and press my uniforms, shine my shoes and generally help around the flat.

In the mess the interests of the Grenadier Guards officers were quite different to those of the Irish Guards. With my fellow officers it was a case of off to the horse races in the afternoon and the greyhounds in the evening. Then, for many, it was back to the mess for poker. Few of them were Grenadier 'Deb's Delights', though they were certainly not queer. I suspect they satisfied themselves whoring at Mrs Jessie Featherstonehaugh's in South Kensington. I went to many horse and dog race meetings, but I'd never been a gambling man and felt a bit out of it. Once a week there was a compulsory mess night dinner, which was convivial.

The majority of the national service Guardsmen were, on the whole, pretty uneducated. That is not to say they were not good chaps who would become good soldiers. They were very loyal and were very much 'The Micks muck in'. But they had their limitations. One of my colleagues was doing his rounds in the early hours of the morning of the guard at Marlborough House when Queen Mary was still living there. He approached one of the guardsmen at his post and asked him whom he thought he was guarding. The reply came: 'I don't rightly know, Sir, but I think it's Queen Victoria.'

On another occasion an Irish lad in my company called Dooley had too much to drink one night and picked a fight in Hyde Park with a perfectly innocent passer-by. The police were called and he was charged with assault. Dooley appeared at Tower Bridge Magistrates Court and it was my job to attend and look after his and the regiment's interests. The presiding magistrate, Miss Sybil Campbell, had a Draconian reputation. However, it was hoped that if Dooley pleaded guilty she could be persuaded to let the Army deal with him. Unfortunately, he was sentenced to six months in jail which shattered him.

It was then my duty to visit Dooley in Brixton Prison. Most of the inmates were on remand and allowed to wear their own clothes. Many seemed to be spivs walking about in camel hair coats. Dooley cut a pathetic figure in an ill-fitting prison-issue coarse, grey flannel uniform. I offered to write to his family in Ireland, but he did not want them to know he was in prison. In my view his punishment did not fit the crime.

When sober, Dooley was – like so many of his fellow Guardsmen – a quiet and simple soul and essentially illiterate. Indeed, in No.1 Company our Clerk was the only one among the ranks who read a newspaper.

Another episode which stood out was a scandal in the Grenadiers when an officer was charged with buggering a Guardsman. His court martial took place in secret at Pirbright, far from the prying press. At this time, adult buggery was still a criminal offence and received much public attention when a prominent Conservative MP, Ian Harvey, was caught buggering a Guardsman in the bushes in St James's Park - a case of 'a Tory at the bottom of a Guardsman' rather than a fairy at the bottom of the garden. Both men were fined five pounds after indecency charges were dropped; Harvey duly left politics and the marital home.

However, the one event of interest was the dock strike of 1949-1950. There had been industrial trouble in the docks before and during the War. And despite there being a Labour government, there was still trouble and a strike had been called which was crippling the country. The troops were called in, but fortunately the fear that we might meet resistance did not materialise. There were not even demonstrations as we drove to our designated dock. The Navy had been drafted in to operate the cranes and we were there to manhandle the cargo into the nets and then into the warehouses. The Navy's crane skills were about as inadequate as our manhandling skills.

In those days, there were no container ships and, apart from bulk cargo for grain or coal, all other imports came in crates or packages. The cargo swayed about interminably at the end of the cranes. Where two experienced dockers could manhandle a huge crate, it took six or seven guardsmen to do the same.

Although we worked extremely hard, our productivity was appalling. Despite two or three times the normal manpower, we only unloaded about one third of what a gang of dockers could achieve. What started out as fun and a challenge, became a very hard slog. Happily, it did not last too long.

Chapter Four

In the spring of 1950 demobilisation loomed and the need to find a job became my prime preoccupation. I had always wanted to work abroad: it seemed from my youthful observations so much more exciting and comfortable with large houses and servants. My grandfather, by now nearly 80, offered me a job in his jobbing firm on the Stock Exchange. As his son Ian had emigrated to Southern Rhodesia (now Zimbabwe) he was hoping that a member of the family would take over. But I had seen him catching the eight thirty train from Tub's Hill every day and returning at five p.m. I was determined that this was not the life for me.

Being based in London, and not very busy, I had plenty of time for interviews. In those days my mother thought that connections were important and to a limited extent they were. Through her connections she got me introductions to ICI, BP, Steel Brothers and BAT. The interview with ICI looked a dead cert, with my Ampleforth education, two Higher School Certificates and a commission in the Irish Guards, together with the fast-tracking of my application by Sir Paul Chambers, who was on the ICI Board.

I marched into the Personnel Officer's room, complete with dark suit, stiff white collar, Brigade tie, bowler hat and tightly furled umbrella. The interviewer had a heavy Scots accent – I suspected he did not like to be leant upon by a Director. Further, in those very egalitarian times after the War, he undoubtedly resented public school boys and had even less time for Brigade of Guards officers. He asked me what I knew about ICI; I did not know much. I said I was hoping to hear from him about the job. But he persisted. Had I read the Annual Report? What did I think of the balance sheet? He could see that I was lost. The interview finished with him dismissing me as typical of my class who thought they were entitled to a managerial job.

At BP in Finsbury Square, it was a more considerate experience. I had an interview with an adviser who had known my father. He charmingly explained that BP only recruited people for their Management Programme, who had been to a first class university and got a good degree. He suggested

I went away, achieved this, and then reapplied. I never did get that degree but, thirty years later, I was invited to join the BP Board.

Steel Brothers was a company that traded in India, Pakistan and Burma, with offices in Italy and London. They agreed to take me as a management trainee without even an interview. After the rebuffs from ICI and BP, this was comforting.

Next on the list was BAT, at that time based at Egham where its head office had been evacuated during the War. I was invited to an interview there with the Head of Personnel, Desmond Misselbrook. He was by repute a psychologist recruited by the then Deputy Chairman, Duncan Oppenheim, to restructure the company's management. He had had a similar role in man management in the Royal Navy, responsible for the selection of naval officers and ratings for particular tasks.

I was encouraged by the first interview because Misselbrook was at pains to explain what BAT was all about and that working abroad for the company would not be all 'moonlight and roses'. Eager for a job, I assured him that these were just the challenges I was seeking. The next step would be to attend a two-day selection board where I would be more fully assessed. An invitation to attend the board at the Oaklands Park Hotel in Weybridge duly arrived. The board was similar to the War Office version without the outdoor exercises. We had talks on BAT which gave an impression that they were trying to deter you from joining. At the end, we were told the result of the board would be known within ten days.

I liked the company's approach to recruitment, particularly after ICI. They did take graduates, but seemed to want non-graduates too and I was keen to join. Their letter arrived but did not say that I had been selected. Rather, it politely invited me to another interview. I was despondent. The interview was to be with one of Misselbrook's assistants, which was not a good omen. In essence, I discovered that BAT wanted to offer me a place on their Management Programme, but thought I was much too grand. I tried to persuade them that not only did I like the prospect of working for BAT, but that I needed the job as I was due to leave the Army. I was told to write to BAT reassuring them that I fully understood what the job was about and that I really wanted it.

A suitably humble letter was written and I received in reply an invitation to join a management trainee course at Egham, due to start two weeks after my demob. When the time came, I was glad to leave, but felt sorry to go. Soldiering was not for me. However, I was immensely proud to have been a Guardsman after my rather sheltered private schooling. It was a stimulating introduction to a cross section of the population. It was in many respects a humbling experience – but disciplined and very worthwhile. Also, I had made many friends whom I was going to miss.

In July 1950 I joined BAT at an annual salary of £350. The company had arranged digs for me in Egham. The course consisted of some twenty trainees; one an Indian who had graduated from Oxford, while the rest were English public schoolboys who had completed their military service. We did not appear to be a very bright lot. The course was held in a very large room which had a glass partition separating it from a typing pool which proved a distraction for both the 'pupils' as we were called and the young female typists.

The course was predominantly about accounting, designed to teach us how a profit and loss and balance sheet were prepared from a company's transactions. It was also to indicate how a company was financed. Our instructor, an accountant called Drummond, was a very good teacher. We also had lectures on leaf growing, cigarette production, buying and selling and purchasing materials. BAT had not embraced marketing at that time. One day we visited the Ardath Tobacco Company in the City of London which BAT had partially acquired in 1925 when it purchased the overseas rights. It was rumoured that the BAT directors were mystified by its profitability – BAT was not allowed to sell cigarettes in the UK – and bought it purely for its export business. This is how they discovered the secret of duty draw down.

Before the course, we had to state our career preferences for sales, production, etc. I chose sales. During the course we were asked about where we would like to work and I selected Brazil. It appealed to me as a large country with great opportunities. We each had to write an analysis of the politics and economic potential of the country we had chosen. By the end of the course I knew more about Brazil through my research than I did about Britain.

The course ended with an exam in accounting. Ironically, the sales people got higher marks than their accounting colleagues, who struggled to even pass. Throughout my forty-five years with BAT, I looked upon that accounting course as the most worthwhile of any training that I undertook.

During the course I became friendly with David Weaver and we both decided to share a car. I had learned to drive in the Army and discovered that a friend of mine in the Harlequins Rugby Club had a red 1924 open-tourer four-seater Humber, which he was willing to sell to us for fourteen pounds. There were clearly a number of imperfections. The difficulty of getting the collapsible hood up, the position of the battery on the running board, the accelerator lodged between the foot brake and the clutch, the rear wheels larger than the front ones and the play in the 'advance and retard' mechanism all made driving unpredictable. Added to these, a previous owner had his registered address as the British Museum. Nevertheless we went ahead and bought it.

We certainly had great fun with the car and it taught me far more about the internal combustion engine than I ever learnt at school. While we didn't need an MOT to prove roadworthiness, we did need insurance. It was possible to get an insurance cover note for six weeks, costing six shillings. A completed application form had to be sent before expiry. We later received a letter at our digs from the insurers declining to insure the car at any price. Thereafter, we survived on a series of cover notes from different insurers. One quoted twenty-five pounds for six months with a ten pound excess. You could buy a better car for that! After the course, I was off to Denmark and David to Liverpool. We managed to sell the car back to its previous owner for fourteen pounds. It was the only time I have ever sold a car for the same price that I paid for it.

BAT had a policy of testing its newly minted managers in near-abroad postings before investing in the expensive business of sending them to the Orient, Africa or South America. The testing was not concerned with your sales or accounting abilities, but whether you would behave in foreign parts. One notable bounder was the actor George Sanders, who was reputed to have misbehaved with married women while a BAT junior manager in Argentina. I suspect that this was hypocritical of the BAT Board, among whom were a sprinkling of womanisers, not least the company's long-time Chairman, Sir Hugo Cunliffe-Owen. So it was entirely in keeping that the company's doctor in Harley Street, Dr Bartleman, was also an eminent VD consultant. I was sent to him for a mundane health check-up.

So, before going to Brazil, I was assigned to the Copenhagen operation. It was explained to me that Copenhagen was chosen to allow me to learn Portuguese there. I was to attend the Berlitz School. Once there, I duly applied only to find out that the curriculum was limited to teaching Danish to the Portuguese. I never did learn Danish or Portuguese. To work in Denmark as a foreigner required a permit but my fellow pupil, Tony Mercer, and I were not granted one, so we were only allowed to observe the company operations. These did not work particularly efficiently. Denmark was suffering from a shortage of foreign exchange. Tobacco was allocated to the two companies on the basis of their pre-War market share and cigarettes were allocated to wholesalers and tobacconists. There was no real competition.

The company had kept its name, American Tobacco, throughout the German occupation and an Englishman, Godfrey Bryant, had retained his position as Chairman and General Manager. A convivial extrovert, and a Danish speaker, he was reputed to have helped the Danish resistance. Bryant's deputy, another Englishman, who spoke immaculate Danish, had also held his position, although he was rumoured to have been an MI6 plant. Sir Duncan Oppenheim confirmed to me many years later that, before the Second World War, BAT was occasionally asked to employ MI6 agents in their overseas operations.

The factory management were a comic pair. Andreason, a Dane, pretended to be an English country gentleman. He only wore tweeds and spoke English with a heavy Danish accent. In contrast, Plasket, an Englishman, dressed like a Dane and spoke Danish with a distinctive estuary accent. Our factory training involved lying among the tobacco bales in the leaf warehouse sleeping off our hangovers. We sometimes accompanied salesmen on their calls which comprised swapping cigarettes allocations for coffee. Both were in short supply. We had desks in the office where we looked at statistics. Curiously for a tobacco company we were not allowed to smoke until after lunch. There was another company manufacturing cigarettes but there was no competition. In subsequent years when tobacco was freely available and competitiveness returned, the BAT business in Denmark had no competitive skills and eventually it was taken over by the competition.

During our stay in Denmark we were visited by McKenzie from personnel who told Mercer the bad news that he was not going to East Africa but to West Africa. I was still destined for Brazil but, in the end, Mercer did go to East Africa and I was sent to West Africa. At least we had not 'blotted our copybooks' in Copenhagen. Before going to Africa we visited BAT headquarters in London for briefing but more importantly were sent for a fortnight to the London School of Tropical Medicine where we learnt about malaria and all the other tropical diseases that were about to afflict us.

Chapter Five

On 1 April 1951 I boarded a BOAC Argonaut at Heathrow, at that time merely a collection of one-storey temporary buildings, and headed for Lagos. The Argonaut was a four piston-engine plane which was a development of the wartime DC6. In today's terms it had a very limited range and provided a deafeningly noisy service.

We stopped at Rome and Tripoli before the long flight across the Sahara to Kano, taking about twenty-four hours in all. My mother had given me, as a farewell present, Graham Green's 'Heart of the Matter', a dark tragedy set in colonial West Africa. I read most of it on the flight. It was pretty depressing.

At Kano we disembarked shortly after dawn and were bussed down a dusty road amid a dry, light brown, scrubby landscape to the terminal. Outside the terminal – a one-room shed with a bar – was a huge pile of empty beer bottles around which vultures were hovering. Inside was littered with unshaven slovenly-dressed expatriates either dozing or drinking. My depression deepened.

My mood wasn't much improved on arrival in Lagos, the Nigerian capital on April Fools' Day 1951 where I was met by the wife of the Director of Prisons. A representative of the BAT travel department, she was a robustly-built lady with a commanding voice and she herded us to the company mess set aside for bachelors. This was a largish house, sparsely furnished. She ordered us to smarten ourselves up before going to head office, a converted warehouse in Lagos, to meet the General Manager. It was all rather intimidating.

The 1st April 1951 was also the Founding Day of the Nigerian Tobacco Company. Hitherto, it had traded as BAT Ltd - the UK company – through a series of agents and rented warehouses. The company also had a manufacturing plant in Ibadan.

In the late 1940s and 50s, Africans in Nigeria and the Gold Coast were clamouring for independence. Part of the colonial government's response was to encourage, via fiscal incentives, local importers and manufacturers to set up subsidiaries. Hence, the Nigerian Tobacco Company. This provoked BAT's directors to look at the prospects of manufacturing cigarettes more widely in

West Africa. They were somewhat embarrassed that these markets had been neglected and by the magnitude of their potential.

The main cause of the neglect was the management arrangements. The Director for African Markets was largely paid by commission on sales – particularly lucrative exports from the UK. After the Second World War, trading companies in West Africa realised the region's potential and rapidly expanded their branch network. These companies included: United African Company of Nigeria [UAC], G.B. Ollivant, John Holt, Compagnie Française de l'Afrique Occidentale, Societe Commerciale de l'Ouest Africain Nigeria and A.G. Leventis.

Since BAT did not realise the potential of the market, cigarettes were often out of stock as supplies were haphazard. With sales expenses being deductable from the Director's commission, there was virtually no sales force and, therefore, no reliable information on market needs was communicated to head office. The trading houses all supplied self-serving and conflicting information.

Alistair Rohrig, an American, was the Director in the late forties. Not only was he greedy, but he also had a reputation of being an unsavoury lecher – pressuring the wives of staff to sleep with him or it would be hard luck for their husbands. Most of the managers valued their jobs.

Even by the standards of the early 1950s, BAT's business practices were pretty basic. Indeed, my six-week induction before going to my posting to the Gold Coast, consisted of travelling around Western Nigeria in a company Standard Vanguard with 'Steady Eddie', a chubby chap with an open face. He was an affable character, popular in all the clubs we visited. With no training in marketing or selling, he did not know much about the business nor did he wish to know. We made the occasional courtesy call on a trading house, but spent most of our time drinking large bottles of beer in numerous European clubs dotted around the region.

'Steady Eddie' was popular in these clubs on account of his considerable repertoire of filthy songs – euphemistically called 'Service' songs by the BBC during the War. He was a member of a club, The Pisspots, which stood for Puritanically In-Service Songs Preservation of the Theme Society. It had been started by the well-known moustachioed comedian Jimmy Edwards. He and some of his friends were outraged when the BBC started playing these songs with clean words.

CHAPTER FIVE

After six weeks in Nigeria I was transferred to the Gold Coast. Here again, the Gold Coast Tobacco Company had been formed on 1st April 1951 to replace BAT. As in Nigeria, the arrangements were the same, with cigarettes distributed through the Gold Coast branches of the same trading companies as in Nigeria. But in the Gold Coast, all the cigarettes were imported, whereas in Nigeria the highest proportion was locally manufactured in Ibadan.

The Gold Coast Tobacco Company's operation consisted of an office in Accra – with a manager and his secretary – and warehouses in the capital and in Takoradi, both rented from and staffed by UAC. We imported two brands from Liverpool: John Player Navy Cut and Churchman's No.1. Both came in airtight tins of fifty cigarettes.

The management house was owned by the company and rather prosaically called Bramtoco. I was to stay with the manager, Dickie Bird, and his wife, Doreen, until a house to rent could be found. Dickie had served on the West Coast for twenty-five years and was an 'Old Coaster'. These people were not stars within the company: Dickie was a worthy soul, more of a 9am to 4pm man who enjoyed a good two hours at home for lunch. He had a marked aversion to travelling up country.

After six weeks, a house was found in the Syrian quarter of Accra (the Lebanese, who were mostly traders, were classed as Syrians). The house was a rambling bungalow in a scruffy yard. It had a large living room, three bedrooms, a bathroom and kitchen. Its cement floors were painted green, while the walls were white except that water from the roof had seeped down and stained them. The electrical wiring was exposed on the walls and crackled alarmingly whenever rain water got through.

Dickie thought that this accommodation would be temporary until the company built its own house. By this time, I had been joined in the house by an accountant and Dickie told us we could spend fifty pounds on furniture and household linen. Even in those days, this was a derisory amount. We were both able to buy a bed and wardrobe, linen and towels, two upright chairs and a refrigerator. Dickie also gave us his termite-eaten carpets that he had kept between the springs of his bed and the mattress. For chairs in the living room, we used three empty forty mille packing cases (designed to hold 40,000 cigarettes) turned upside down.

We had to eat out about two miles away at the Accra European Club.

This was a somewhat tired institution on the edge of the commercial and administrative centre. It was a club exclusively for Europeans: no Africans, no Syrians, no Indians and no Americans (as some could have been black). To become a member of the club you had to be twenty-one. I was only twenty, but as I needed to eat somewhere, I filled in twenty-one on my application form.

That the recently-elected Assembly – the hub of Gold Coast nationalism and housed on the opposite side of the road – allowed this offensively-titled and constituted club to co-exist was an indication of the tolerance of Gold Coast Africans towards the prejudices of Europeans. During the nearly two years that I spent in the Gold Coast, there was an even louder clamour for independence and not just self-rule. I recall only politeness and cheerfulness from the population, never resentment.

Shortly before I arrived in Accra, Kwame Nkrumah and his closest colleagues were released from jail where they had been incarcerated for political misdemeanours. It had been a futile attempt to stem the tide of nationalism. Martyrs inside jail were much more effective in disrupting the country, and therefore the economy, than those agitating outside.

In the early 1950s, sterling was in crisis and the sterling area needed all the dollars it could muster. The Gold Coast's cocoa and gold were significant sources of dollars. If independence kept the natives quiet and the dollars flowing, then it had to be accelerated. Originally, the leisurely timetable was for Nigerian independence first, followed by the Gold Coast. But because of the sterling crisis, priority was given to the Gold Coast.

Nkrumah and his party seized the initiative. Released on 12 February 1951, still wearing his PG (Prison Graduate) Forage cap, he was asked the following day to form a government as Chief Minister. Within a year, all the ministers' houses had been built and Black Power, supported by a largely-expatriate administration, was a reality. Exports flourished and the economy boomed. In March 1952, by now PM, he presented his 'motion of destiny' for full independence.

Cigarette trading was concerned with ensuring sufficient supply met the demand for a fresh product. Even in airtight tins of fifty, cigarettes had a limited life. When cigarettes are stale, the paper is discoloured and spotted and the smoke becomes harsh or very acrid. Even in so-called vacuum-sealed tins, there is some air and some moisture in the tobacco. The rise and fall in temperature, so prevalent in the Tropics, causes the tobacco to sweat or dry out.

Demand was very seasonal – increasing by some twenty per cent to thirty per cent in the cocoa season. The bigger circumference Churchman's No.1 particularly increased in demand: they were more expensive and, thus, more prestigious. But they also came in a bigger tin, which was popular with farmers, who could cram more banknotes inside as they buried their savings in the ground.

The trading houses could not have cared less about freshness: they were only interested in turnover. If cigarettes were abundant in supply, the trading houses used them as loss leaders. If supplies were short, they used them for conditional selling.

For some time since the War, cigarettes had been in short supply and the market was disorderly; shortages in some areas, over-supply in others, no stock control, stale stock and fluctuating prices. The task of the Gold Coast Tobacco Company was to bring about order. My role was to go around the country visiting the trading houses and the street markets to assess the supply situation, buy back any stale old stock and try to ensure that prices were constant and at the desired level. My journey covered the triangle of Accra, Kumasi and Takoradi, with the occasional trip to Togoland [about 120 miles to the east of Accra]. My only staff was a small, neat and quietly-spoken driver called Bismark, who came from that part of Togoland that was formerly German.

Working the street markets was generally genial with lots of laughter and inquisitive chat. Sometimes it was rather grim when one came across people who had gross deformities such as elephantiasis, or the stub limbs and hollow faces of lepers. Some of the lepers sold cigarettes and I unquestionably avoided them for fear of contagion. I felt unkind and uncomfortable about this. On a lighter note, when Albert Schweitzer died in 1965, The Observer newspaper included this joke in his obituary. Two cannibals were watching a blonde lady stew in a cooking pot. One turned to the other and said: 'I prefer my breakfast in bed.'[1]

1 However it could be this. 'What did the cannibal say when he came upon a sleeping missionary? Ah! Breakfast in bed!'

One charming aspect throughout the Ashanti region was the children yelling "Kwesi" [Sunday] as you passed. Most boys were called after the day of the week that they were born on: UN Secretary General Annan was born on a Friday, hence his first name is "Kofi". The inference of Sunday was that it was the day 'the white man' did not go to work, so they assumed it was his birthday.

The managers of the trading houses were less welcoming. Turnover was king – and their bonuses were linked with it – and cigarettes made a major contribution to turnover. They were really not concerned about over-stocking the market. But for the Gold Coast Tobacco Company this was a major problem. My role, and that of the manager, was to grip the chaotic market situation. We were not popular.

Mostly when travelling up country I stayed at the UAC rest houses or, at times, with the branch managers. A lot of the older managers had been on the coast for years and seen huge changes, particularly in the relationship between Africans and Europeans. Instead of Europeans becoming closer to Africans as the clamour for independence grew, one quite senior branch manager became convinced that the very opposite had occurred.

He attributed this to the arrival of the wives of expatriates. Before the War, because of the unhealthy climate, very few wives or children went to the Gold Coast. Tours were then of twenty-one months' duration. Naturally, the great majority of expatriates had black mistresses. These paramours did not live openly in government or company houses in the expatriate areas but visited their partners in the night. Through these mistresses the expatriates were able to tap into all the news, gossip and intrigue that preoccupied the Africans in the local town and the district. The mistresses, in turn, reported back on business and government news. His hypothesis was that with the arrival of wives this informal network collapsed and distrust between the two communities grew, making the demand for self-government more urgent.

Shortly after I arrived in Accra, the company decided to replace the fifties' airtight tins with tens' shell-and-slide packings for John Player's Navy Cut This was not popular, but as we had a monopoly, it was successful. As far as I was concerned there was a downside. As the sea splashed on the packing cases being manhandled through the surf, more cigarettes became contaminated by the water as the bitumen wrappers were not nearly as effective as the old airtight tins. As a result, hundreds of thousands of cigarettes had to be destroyed. It was not dissimilar to burning cash. It was a time-consuming, tedious management job and I spent hours in the sun supervising it.

I arrived one evening in Hoe Hoe, Togoland to find the district in mourning over the death that day of their Chief. The following afternoon my driver, Bismark, approached me and asked if he could sleep on his mat in my bedroom. It was the custom, he explained, for one or two strangers to be slaughtered and buried with the Chief to assist him in the next world. Bismark was just such a stranger.

After six months the Gold Coast government introduced the Pioneer Industries Act to encourage manufacturers to set up local factories and make the country less dependent on imports. The incentives were exceedingly generous and needed to be because the import of cigarettes was extremely profitable. BAT not only made a high margin on its costs before duty drawback, but when drawback was added the profit was even more lucrative.

Drawback was introduced in the early days of manufactured cigarettes when duty on tobacco was very low. Tobacco was imported at eight per cent to ten per cent moisture content, while cigarettes were exported at twelve to fourteen per cent moisture content. It was the weight of tobacco, including the moisture, on which duty was paid. On importing the tobacco for manufacturing with eight per cent moisture content it was lighter than when exported in cigarettes with twelve per cent content. Duty was paid on the lighter weight and reclaimed on the heavier weight.

With the rates of duty very low, the amounts gained from drawback were not great. But as rates became higher, drawback became a very significant element in the profits of export manufacturers. So much so that, just before drawback was abolished when Britain joined the European Common Market in 1973, there was more profit in invoicing Super King size cigarettes at the same price as Regular size. What is more, when filter-tipped cigarettes became popular, the smaller the filter – hence the more tobacco involved – the more profitable the product. The UK was the only significant cigarette-exporting country offering manufacturers this competitive advantage.

BAT's calculations showed that the Pioneer Industries Act was so generous that its excise reductions on locally-made cigarettes were such that they could be sold very profitably at half the price of imported cigarettes, although they were still not as lucrative as imported brands.

A strategy was therefore proposed to determine whether there was a consumer population that could not afford imported cigarettes, but could be attracted to lower-priced local manufacturers. Preferably the two markets – imported and locally-produced – should be kept apart geographically.

I was consulted on a suggested North of the Cocoa Belt area where there was a sizeable population which was much poorer and which might welcome such a product. I was commissioned to develop a marketing plan for the new company. At the same time, Dickie Bird was told that when he returned from leave all his time should be spent acquiring a site for a factory close to the port of Takoradi.

Apart from local manufacture, there was an obligation on the company to develop Gold Coast leaf tobacco and Frank Burden, most of whose experience had been in the Far East, was posted to Accra to survey the country and establish experimental plots.

Once Dickie had gone on leave, I moved into his house. After living in a house in the Syrian quarter, it was a luxury indeed. With a cook called Napoleon, who was from French Togoland, and two house boys, there was no need for meals at the Accra [European Club]. I entertained extravagantly and, from time to time, Frank Burden came to stay. He was a much older man, congenial and very stout with a phenomenal capacity for gin and whisky. On a Saturday or Sunday he would regularly drink a bottle of gin at lunch followed by a bottle of whisky in the evening. Even in the hard-drinking Gold Coast, many thought this feat unbelievable. On condition that they stayed the course, I invited some friends to witness Frank demolishing his requisite two bottles of spirits.

By the time Dickie returned from leave, Hampson, the Chief Executive of the Cocoa Marketing Board [CMB], who had worked with my father in Germany, offered to rent to the company a vacant CMB house which was completely furnished. It was assigned to me. Burden, by now, was spending much of his time in the country – a lot of it 'in the bush', leaf growing. For this he was based in Accra and in my house.

I then went on a month-long trip around the north of the country, motoring via Kumasi to Takoradi, then on to the western border, followed by the northern and eastern borders and down to northern Togoland and back to Accra. After Tamale there were no catering rest houses, only empty, thatched, brown mud houses without windows, running water or electricity. Prior to leaving I had bought a range of camping equipment in Accra along with a primus stove and a couple of Tilley lamps. More importantly, I had brought with me from London a portable lavatory seat to avoid the indignity and dangers from bouts of squatting! However, I had assumed that my steward boy, an Ibo from Eastern Nigeria, knew how to light a Tilley lamp. By the time we had ruined two mantles, we resigned ourselves to coping in the darkness. As a 'boxwallah' which was slang for all of us in commerce, I was certainly not prepared to ask for help from the District Commissioner when I dined with him that night.

The DC urged me to visit a scheme designed to eradicate river blindness in the upper reaches of the Volta River on the Eastern border. It was evident from the deserted villages one came across that this disease was a scourge. The seasonal rise and fall in the Volta covered a considerable area. When the river fell, the silt soil on the flooded area was extremely fertile. Unfortunately, the farmers could only plant small areas as the rest was covered with wild shrubs in which the river fly bred and thrived.

The solution was a cash crop which could be planted and harvested in between flood seasons. The manager of the project believed that tobacco was a suitable crop. In Nigeria this flood land was known as Fadima and good tobacco was grown on it.

At Bolgatanga the rest house was located on a knoll outside the town. I was worried that there were lions in the area and, indeed, I heard roars in the night, albeit some way off. This was compensated by the arrival in the morning of provocatively shaped bare-breasted, dusky maidens delivering water. Very arousing!

Another feature of life in this region was the White Fathers doing their missionary work. Their flocks were immense and their cheerful dedication was exemplary. We grumbling expatriates on twenty-one-month tours could only admire how happy these Fathers were, even though they did nine or ten years before going on leave.

At that time in some outlying part of the northern region, the cowrie shell, not cash, formed the currency. There was an unofficial rate of exchange in the main town and one of the responsibilities of the DC was to ensure that this was not devalued by unscrupulous traders from the coast dumping a lot of cowrie shells in the market. In such a primitive economy it was clear to me that even low-priced cigarettes were not going to find a big market.

While in Accra, I submitted my marketing plan. One of my recommendations was the introduction of a low-priced brand called Tusker, which was still on the market in Ghana when I retired in 1995. Meanwhile, Dickie Bird was concentrating on piloting through an application for Pioneer status under the Act and, more importantly, securing the site for the new factory near Takoradi. A somewhat intimidating main board director, Deputy Chairman Fritz Bodde, monitored progress. A Dutchman in every way with a booming voice and a no nonsense manner, he and his party, accompanied by Dickie, went to inspect the proposed site.

After tramping around the uncleared bush site for an hour or so in the midday sun, one of the party checked the numbers on the ground survey markers with the map, only to discover that they were on the wrong piece of land. For three months Dickie had been looking at the wrong site. There was a certain *froideur* at the company cocktail party held at Dickie's house that night. He was later transferred to East Africa where he spent the rest of his career as an office manager. Shortly after completing my report I went on leave.

While I had been in the Gold Coast the clamour for independence had become more urgent, but there were problems on the economic front. The main difficulty was with the rapid spread of swollen shoot disease on the cocoa farms. At that time the only remedy was to cut down the infected trees and replant. Up to self-government, this was the policy rigorously pursued by the colonial administration, but it was not popular with farmers. Although they received some compensation from the CMB, it was nowhere near sufficient to maintain their income while the new trees were coming into fruit.

Nkrumah accused the colonial government of deliberately impoverishing the farmers and campaigned for the abolition of 'cutting out'. He duly got his way. But, by the late 1960s and Seventies, all the cocoa trees in a huge area around Koforidua had died. Impoverished, the population diminished and in the 1990s, when I last visited Ghana, the land had reverted to largely uncultivated bush. In agriculture there is rarely such a solution as a quick fix.

On the political front, Nkrumah was determined to undermine the authority of every institution including the traditional tribal institutions which worked alongside the colonial administration. He wanted to replace these with a one-party state. As with his cocoa policy, he succeeded in the short term. But the one-party state would prove incompetent and corrupt and in the longer term led to an ungovernable Ghana.

Chapter Six

I was on leave in the early months of 1953 at a time when foreign exchange for holidays was rationed to twenty-five pounds per person per year. As an overseas visitor I was entitled to fifty pounds which I spent on Alpine skiing trips to St Anton and Kitzbuhl. However, while on leave I was summoned to head office to discuss my marketing plan for the Gold Coast. The powers-that-be were pleased with my findings and offered me the job of marketing manager of the Pioneer Tobacco Company and the chance to implement my recommendations with the proviso that first the factory had to be built and equipped. In the meantime I was to work with the Nigerian Tobacco Company [NTC] until production in the Gold Coast could begin in nine months' time.

When my leave ended I was sent to Onitsha, then the largest town in eastern Nigeria. For administrative and political reasons, Nigeria was divided into three regions: north, east and west. North of the Niger River, the Hausa tribe were dominant, while in the East the Ibos prevailed and in the rest of the country the Yoruba tribe were the most influential. None of them liked being ruled in this way and each wanted a larger share of the federal cake. There were numerous other smaller tribes who also resented the regional set-up. All of them wanted the colonial government out as soon as possible and were frustrated by the slow pace of change. It was not a happy political scene though, for the year I was in Nigeria, little violence was evident.

The NTC had a number of houses designed for bachelors with a limited number of rooms, arising from the fact that the company policy prescribed that expatriates could only marry after two tours of duty – in effect, after four years. This policy was enforced by only paying the marriage allowance – around forty per cent extra – after four years and by not paying air fares for wives. However, James Murphy, who had been at Ampleforth with me, defied this policy and, after just one tour, brought his wife to Nigeria at his own expense. It was not long after that the shortcomings of this policy changed.

The company's bachelor house in Onitsha where I was billeted suffered from two major disadvantages, both stemming from the decision to build it on the wrong site. Firstly, there was no air conditioning and we slept under mosquito nets with the windows open. Unfortunately, the roof was infested with bats which swarmed through the windows and fluttered against the mosquito netting. The only solution was to swat the bats with a tennis racquet and, after they disappeared, close the windows and then sweat profusely all night.

Secondly, there was a bush track running alongside the property's fence. This turned out to be a very busy thoroughfare linking the Onitsha market with nearby villages. From early each morning there was a constant shuttle of mammies who stopped to pee or defecate on their way to the market.

My job in Onitsha was very similar to my earlier work in the Gold Coast, although there were not so many cigarettes to be destroyed. What was different – apart from the people – was the geography, particularly in the Niger Delta where the great river branches into a myriad of tributaries before reaching the sea. In the days before outboard motors, canoes were needed to reach many outstations as well as, in places, to cross the Niger itself. Idah in my area was on the opposite bank of the Niger and to reach it by canoe took nearly two hours. The crew of two had to paddle upstream for nearly an hour before setting off across the fast flowing stream to Idah.

While on leave, and knowing that I was going to Nigeria, I had bought a copy of Mary Kingsley's 'Travels in West Africa' [1897]. It was a refreshing read. She actually enjoyed West Africa, believing Europeans once there should dress as if they were in Piccadilly. She wore black crinoline dresses and a hat and carried an elegant parasol. She either walked or went by canoe, eschewed staying with missionaries or DCs, preferring to lodge with villagers even when they were known to be cannibals.

One of her many feats was to climb the 13,350-ft Mount Cameroon. If she could do it, I was determined to do it too. The Coronation of Queen Elizabeth II was coming up and there was to be a long holiday and Mount Cameroon was in my area. I proposed to the sales manager, Tom Slack, that I should combine business with pleasure: visiting the markets in the Cameroons but spending the long weekend of the Coronation climbing the mountain. He enthusiastically bought into my idea but insisted on joining me and a colleague, Freddie Almond, on the climb.

We met up in Victoria on the Friday and had a convivial evening in the small club there. While many District Officers climbed up and down in a day, we planned to start at midday on the Saturday and spend the night in a hut at 10,000 feet and proceed to the summit on Sunday morning, returning to Victoria in the evening. Few, if any, of the people in the club had attempted the feat and there was the distinct impression that boxwallahs like us from Lagos did not know what we were in for and were doomed to fail.

We arranged for a guide and four porters to carry our sleeping bags and food to the hut. We also took along some champagne to celebrate reaching the summit. After an early lunch, we set off from Buea, an administrative town at about 3,000 feet which has the highest rainfall in West Africa and, therefore, is one of the wettest places in the world. It rained heavily and incessantly as we clambered and struggled up the path in the tropical rain forest. Tom was rather pleased with his plastic all-embracing cape, until we stopped for a break after an hour and he revealed himself to be as wet as the rest of us from sweating.

Our porters had no difficulty in jogging up to the hut and were there before we arrived. The hut was above the tree line but in the clouds; it was, however, dry and comfortable. We set off early the next morning and reached the summit by 10am. There we drank our champagne, all the while in dense cloud with no view at all. We were back in the hut for lunch at 1pm. We lingered over lunch, confident that the descent would be easier than the ascent. It wasn't.

The rain was intense. The path was a muddy stream down which we slipped and slithered, sometimes on our feet, sometimes on our bottoms and backs. It was slow going and we eventually reached Buea well after dark. Utterly exhausted, we retired to the rest house in Victoria. It had been our intention on the Monday morning to enter the club triumphantly to confound the sceptics. However, we were so bruised and stiff we had to lick our wounds. On Tuesday we did manage to hobble and limp into the club. Expecting to be heartily congratulated, we were instead greeted by the news that Mount Everest had been climbed!

A month or so after I returned to Onitsha, Tom informed me that I would not be joining the Pioneer Tobacco Company as planned, but would be going to Port Harcourt as the NTC's Eastern Region Manager. It was a great disappointment. Apparently, Frank Burden who was to be the general manager there and who had stayed with me many times, thought I was too 'uppity'. It was not a reason I could accept and I sent in my resignation.

The management in Lagos were told by London to talk me out of it. I was summoned to Lagos and told that while the decision could not be reversed, I had a great future with BAT and London had exciting plans for me. I withdrew my resignation, partly persuaded by the 'sweet talk', and partly dissuaded by the humbling prospect of seeking a new job.

So Port Harcourt was the immediate prospect. It was a purpose-built town, the second largest in the densely populated eastern region. The administrative capital, Enugu, the largest town and market, was the seat of the regional government which covered all the territories south of the Benue River and east of the Niger, including the eastern part of the Niger Delta and the British Cameroons.

The dominant Ibo tribe were mostly Catholic although around Calabar there were other tribes who had been converted to Protestantism. All in all, the West Africa coast was predominantly Christian in contrast to the Muslims in the north. The Christian missionaries had done a good job educating the Africans. The Ibos were particularly adept at adopting Western ideas and used this knowledge to become clerks and managers throughout government and business all over Nigeria. At this time, the tensions between the Christian Ibos and the Hausa Muslims were dormant. But as the wily, clever Ibos came to dominate trade and the more lucrative administrative and managerial positions, resentment grew and finally erupted in the Biafran War of the late 1960s.

NTC's eastern region was larger than that covered by the government and included the western part of the Niger Delta around Benin. At that time the major export crop was palm oil. BP and Shell together were exploring for oil at a base camp at Owerri in the heart of Igboland. In 1953 they announced a major discovery at Eket and no one at that time realised the huge potential of Nigerian oil or of the profoundly disruptive effect its ownership would have on the country, another cause of the Biafran War.

For some years BAT/NTC had stationed a representative in Port Harcourt. The house was a spacious, well-designed bungalow with a garage and well-kept garden. It came with a cook, a house boy and a gardener. There were some 200 expatriate families in Port Harcourt and it was a more sociable town than Onitsha and possibly had the best golf course in Nigeria, which had been built in 1928. My office, in contrast to the genteel residential area, was in the centre of the African part of town.

It was here that I met Michael Bonfield who became an incomparable friend. Michael was working for the salt division of ICI, which was based in Cheshire. He had been sent to Nigeria to market dendritic salt. ICI wanted to capture the market for ordinary salt with their dendritic product which was more aerated. As the retailers bought salt in big bags by weight and sold it in measures of airtight fifty cigarettes tins, the consumer got a full tin of salt – whether dendritic or not – for the same price. But the weight of the dendritic was considerable less, giving the retailer a much greater profit. It was a 'win win' situation for ICI and the trade but not so good for the consumer.

There were days when Michael and his team were at one end of the market with his loudspeaker van promoting dendritic salt, and I had my team at the other end promoting Galleon, the low-priced cigarette. My work in the eastern region was very similar to what I did in the Gold Coast and Onitsha with the additional responsibility of managing the representative in Onitsha. On a visit to Aba market, where I was checking on distribution and freshness of our cigarettes, I was amused at a mammy surprised at my asking her questions in her Ibo language. "Ah, masser," she said, "you speak our language. You must be a missionary!" "Me no missionary," I replied. "Then you must sleep with one of our ladies!" She was wrong on both counts.

The cigarette business in Nigeria had an association with missionaries because the thin, roll-your-own cigarettes mostly sold in the Muslim north were called Bookie - where the Book part stood for the Bible. This arose because the British and Foreign Bible Society used to distribute copies which were printed on thin, rice paper, ideal also for hand-rolled cigarettes. Legend has it that it was some time before the Society discovered that it was not a plethora of Christian converts in the Muslim north that was responsible for the strong demand for Bibles!

Michael stayed with me whenever he was in Port Harcourt. We played a lot of golf together, drank a lot of beer and got to know each other very well. Michael and his elder brother, Brian, were born in Kenya, but their father deserted them, leaving his family destitute. They returned to England where their relatives rallied round and helped their mother, Alison, with their education.

After the War, the brothers both went to university. Brian became a barrister, while Michael joined the Colonial Service and was posted to Nigeria. There, as an Assistant District Officer [ADO], he had an affair with his boss's wife, which was not on and he was asked to leave the Service, and subsequently joined ICI.

I recall spending an evening with a couple of ADOs who were back from a tour of the bush on foot and bicycle. Their pay was two-thirds of mine. I also had a car and a driver and a comfortable bungalow. By contrast, they had university degrees – which I did not – and bicycles and lived in bush rest houses. BAT was expanding in Africa and elsewhere, but the prospects for the Colonial Service was one of rapidly-shrinking opportunities. Why, I asked, had they not gone for a business career? Business, they had been led to believe, was unethical – such was the liberal attitude post war. No wonder British business waned in the fifties and sixties.

Called to head office in Lagos, I was told to go on leave early, prior to being transferred: my destination would be revealed later when I visited head office in Millbank, London. I was not sorry to leave Nigeria, but sad to be saying goodbye to my driver Samson, who had taken me many thousands of miles over hundreds of days. A quietly-spoken man, he was self-reliant and unfailingly polite with a wry sense of humour. Like me, he was a Catholic and a devout one. He surprised me one day when he revealed he was about to marry a second wife. "But the Church does not agree to a man having two wives," I argued. "How many wives a man has is African palaver, not Church palaver," he replied. Amen. Samson was later killed in the Biafran War – *Requiescat in pace.*

I saw quite a bit of Michael Bonfield while on leave in England. I got to know his mother, brother and step-father Harvey, all of whom became life-long friends. Michael and I went on a golfing tour of Scotland, playing St Andrews, Muirfield and Gullane. Then, you could arrange a tee time at St Andrews' Old Course the evening before and not months in advance as is the case today. I recall a notice by the first tee: 'Four-ball golf should not take longer than three hours' and it didn't.

Michael was also planning a two-week tour of the continent. I agreed to go to Paris with him for the first weekend and we had an extravagant time going to the Folies Bergère and other cabaret spots, eating well, drinking a lot of wine and chatting up lovelies. The outcome was that Michael had no money for the rest of his trip and we returned to London together!

Chapter Seven

On my way to Millbank I was told that I was going to Abyssinia (later renamed Ethiopia in 1963 by Emperor Haile Selassie). It was explained to me that BAT had just won the contract to manage the tobacco monopoly there and I was to be the Sales Manager. It sounded like promotion. I was not sure where Abyssinia was; I nursed the hope that it was near Europe and that I was escaping from Africa. I was mixing it up with Albania. When I got home and discovered where Abyssinia was I was somewhat disappointed. Nobody in head office had been to Addis Ababa, so there was no briefing. I merely called into Millbank to collect my ticket and the 'safe hand' mail for one of BAT's subsidiaries, the Eastern Company in Cairo.

That year, 1954, saw mounting tension between Britain and Egypt with the possibility that British investments there would be seized. The company was concerned that its mail would be read by the Egyptian Secret Police, hence the 'safe hand' I was carrying.

To get to Addis Ababa I first had to fly overnight to Cairo and then on to Abyssinia the next day with Ethiopian Air Lines Inc. On arrival in Cairo, I was asked to disembark on my own before any of the other passengers. My initial reaction was that Egyptian Security suspected me of carrying 'safe hand' but at the terminal the general manager of the Eastern Company was waiting to greet me and relieve me of the mail. The Eastern Company was one of BAT's largest and most profitable subsidiaries and was indeed seized by the Egyptians after the Suez invasion in 1956. At Addis Ababa, I was met by Don Hunt, the BAT general manager of the Imperial Ethiopian Tobacco Monopoly [IETM].

Addis Ababa was where it all happened. The city was built on the slopes of the Entoto Hills, some 8,000 feet above sea level. Set in a forest of eucalyptus trees which were planted in the 1920s and which, in the early days of the city's development, provided fuel for heating and cooking, Addis Ababa's upper parts were riven by deep gullies, infested at night by howling, scavenging hyenas, which roused the hundreds of domestic and stray dogs into a cacophony of barking.

The Imperial Palace and its considerable grounds, which included the cages for the Imperial lions (Emperor Haile Selassie was the Lion of Judah), and the Imperial Ethiopian Racecourse were situated on the upper slopes. At the bottom of the slope there was an extensive plain, housing a railway station, airport, the few industries, a prison, four-star hotels, the Russian Hospital and the IETM factory.

The elite and expatriates inhabited large villas dotted around the hills. We lived by the cathedral near the centre of town in a house that BAT rented from a General. It was located on the edge of a gully which filled up each evening with a pack of howling hyenas. We had a servant each and the mess had its own cook boy.

The major countries had extensive embassy compounds on the outskirts of Addis Ababa. Around the city's main square were a few ten storey buildings. There was one street largely occupied by Armenian jewellers who had been offered refuge in Ethiopia after the genocidal activities of the Ottomans in the First World War. The city was a hive of Tej, bars-cum-brothels. Occasionally, the Emperor could be seen in his large Rolls-Royce, complete with huge pennant, Imperial guards and military escort. As he approached, Ethiopians had to get down from their *garis* [horse taxis], taxis or cars and kneel by the roadside and lower their heads. Europeans were excused from kneeling, but had to get out of their cars and bow.

On one occasion, a Canadian friend, who was Head of the FAO mission, did not get out of his car. So, the Emperor stopped the Rolls and sent an equerry to summon him. My friend immediately complied, bowing in the process. The Emperor then drove off. He had made his point.

There was a curfew every night from midnight to five a.m. Occasionally there were public hangings, most involving bandits. Justice was swift: if they were caught on Monday, they were tried on Tuesday, hanged on Wednesday and buried the next day. Hangings took place in the market and were attended by thousands of spectators. I never went.

On the whole, travelling was reasonably safe, though when near the Danakil country, it could be hazardous. In the Danakil or Afar tribe, you were not a man until you had killed another man and presented your victim's testicles to your bride to be. Fortunately, black testicles were more valuable than those of a white man. With this in mind, when travelling near the Danakil country with the Director of the Regie, I noticed he kept a loaded revolver on the seat between us.

I had been transferred to Ethiopia to work as the IETM's Sales Manager. At the instigation of A. Besse & Co (Aden) Ltd., BAT had been awarded a five year management contract. A. Besse & Co was a trading company operating in and out of Aden and its founder, a Frenchman called Antonin Besse, was the main man in Aden. Through trading and acquiring the Shell agency among others, he made an enormous amount of money – more than enough to endow St Anthony's College, Oxford, in 1950. For a while, Besse had an intense relationship with Freya Stark, the remarkable woman traveller who wrote many books on the Middle East.

Since BAT was among A. Besse & Co's distributorships in Aden and the protectorate, the company agreed to appoint A. Besse as its sole distributor for the whole of Ethiopia. The IETM was an offshoot of the country's Ministry of Finance, which was the most powerful government department. As employees of this Ministry, BAT's staff were able to travel freely throughout Ethiopia, whereas most foreigners including top diplomats needed permits.

The IETM had two organisations. Firstly, the Regie which issued the excise stamps for each cigarette packet, and which licensed wholesalers and retailers. Secondly, the factory which imported tobacco and manufactured cigarettes and distributed them. BAT had won a management contract for operating the factory which had been built in the late 1940s. The first contract had gone to some local Greeks, but they had been convicted of embezzlement and were languishing in the jail over the road from the factory.

There was a small Board comprised of Ethiopians, with a Polish financial adviser. The Director of the Regie and the General Manager of the factory reported to the board. Needless to say, the board had no business experience, but were very interested in profits, although they had no idea how these accrued. So much so, that when we wanted to increase sales, they insisted that smoking was against the traditions of the country. 'More profit but not more sales' was their attitude. They pointed to what they believed to be a passage in the Bible's Orthodox New Testament (Ethiopian version) that stated 'on the death of Christ the earth was dark and the tobacco plants nearby withered and died'.

When BAT began its contract, the factory was producing ten million cigarettes a month. There was one brand, Ketase Work Gold Leaf. BAT initially provided five managers: Don Hunt, the General Manager and

Factory Manager, Sam Dodds, Chief Accountant, Silvio Carbone, Assistant Accounting, Harry Armistead, Leaf Manager, and me, running sales.

Dodds was just under two years from retirement and had recently married a senior nurse at the British Hospital in Addis Ababa. He had previously served in the Far East. Dodds was always tired and spent most of his time dozing or worrying about his health. Carbone, a very competent, helpful and ever-cheerful Italian, did most of his work. Armistead was three or four years older than me and had served with the Ghurkhas in India before joining BAT. He learned about leaf growing in India. At that time, he was, like me, a bachelor. He mostly took himself rather seriously and had a ponderous sense of humour. But he knew his job and took great pride in his work and the tobacco he grew. He was very self-reliant and quite at home living alone in the bush for long periods of time. He had to be, for the leaf growing area was some 200 miles south of Addis Ababa, about a third of the way to the Kenyan border.

When Armistead arrived in Sidamo, he found a chaotic situation: there was no structured relationship between the landlords and the IETM. Nobody knew how much leaf was grown, the quality was atrocious and there was no house or leaf station (storage, buying building or office). Within a year, he had introduced a system of leaf development, built a compound and warehouse, and constructed a charming bungalow made of mud and wattle with a thatched roof.

One of the ingredients of BAT's success outside Europe and North America, was the local cultivation of local leaf. However in countries where land ownership by foreigners was a highly emotional, even revolutionary, issue, BAT never owned tobacco farms. Instead BAT's system was to contract farmers to grow tobacco, providing them with an extension service which showed them the best way to grow it, while also arranging for them to obtain fertiliser, farm tools and credit from local banks. This was a daunting task in Sidamo. The peasant farmers were very primitive: they ploughed the earth by hand with two long poles though there were cattle, donkeys and mules. When Armistead bought a wheelbarrow to move earth in building his house, they queued up to take turns for the excitement of using it.

The tobacco they grew was an oriental variety, which is normally a smallish plant with leaves the size of a child's hand. However, the oriental plant they were producing was about eight feet high with leaves three feet long, with no body, poor taste and little nicotine. At the same time, nobody knew who the farmers were or where they were. Armistead set out recruiting and training leaf assistants and started to register farmers, so gaining their confidence by offering help and undertaking to buy their tobacco. He was greatly encouraged by the response of the farmers. When they had grown and cured their crops, he began purchasing them, area by area, at good prices according to quality.

The first two days purchasing was brisk and everybody was happy. However, on the morning of the third day, the landlords appeared and, using thorny bushes, built a Zareba between the buying station and the road and tracks leading to it. The farmers were escorted by armed men to the Zareba where agents of their landlords demanded seventy-five per cent of their cash receipts, the equivalent to the tariff on crops that the landlords extorted from farmers for the use of their land. This was the brutal economic reality of feudalism.

At first, the farmers refused to pay and appealed to Armistead to intervene. He was told not to interfere in the customs of the country. As there was no food, water or shelter where they were being held, the farmers paid up. Word quickly got around and in the following days no tobacco was brought in for sale. Armistead hurried to Addis Ababa and presented the problem to a hastily convened Board meeting. Eventually a compromise was reached, but it was still a rip-off and the farmers' enthusiastic co-operation in improving the quality of the crop was never again the same.

I used to stay with Armistead when working the markets to the south of his area. On one visit, knowing that he spoke little Galla or Amharic, I asked him whom there was to talk to other than his dog Whisky. There were some American Seventh Day Adventist missionaries nearby, but they kept themselves to themselves. Even though they were against smoking and drinking, they were in favour of tobacco as a cash crop. As to Britons, there was the Consulate at Mega, some 400 miles to the south, near the Kenyan border. In a town about 100 miles away, there was a Briton employed as a senior officer in the Ethiopian Police Force.

Armistead had met him when he called on him when returning from leave. The officer had been in the Burma Police and, on independence, the new government had compelled him to retire. But with his very small pension, he had had to take the job in Ethiopia to pay for his children's education in England. His salary was not high, but neither were his living expenses onerous.

To save as much as possible, he never left his station. So, he was more than somewhat surprised when I called in on him. After chatting about this and that, he mentioned that he had joined the Burma Police in the mid 1920s. I wondered whether he knew my father. "John Sheehy?", he repeated wistfully. "Good God. Is he married with children?"

Later IETM decided to grow Virginia Leaf at Awash. Mike Martineau, with extensive experience in growing leaf in Uganda, came and joined us. Apart from being a good 'leaf man', he was an ebullient sex maniac. With his cheerful and gregarious nature, it took him no time at all to get friendly and intimate with the wives of some of the Swedish Air Force officers stationed at Bishoftu, close to his home base at Lake Awash. On one occasion he received a telephone call at ten p.m. from one of his Swedish lovers urgently requesting him come to see her as she was in trouble with something he had given her. Since he had crashed a number of IETM vehicles and was forbidden to drive, he begged me to drive him the thirty miles to Bishoftu, to which I reluctantly agreed.

He left me outside the house for an hour. When he returned to the car he was very reticent. "Well, what was her problem?" I asked. He replied: "The last time I slept with her she caught a bad cold." "So what took you so long?" I naturally enquired. "Well, I slept with her again!"

On one of his subsequent leaves, Mike decided to get married. I was invited to the wedding and, at the lunch beforehand, he suggested to me that he forget the wedding and that we both take off to Paris. I persuaded him otherwise. Sadly, a few years later, he and his wife were both killed in a road crash in Uganda. He was the greatest fun to be with and very good at his job getting farmers to grow tobacco in inhospitable areas.

A 'Virginia' leaf expert who occasionally visited us was Mr Buwalda, a Dutchman, who spent most of his career growing tobacco in Indonesia. On one of his visits to the Sudan, this very distinguished looking middle-aged European arrived at Khartoum to find all the hotels and the company rest house full. The only room available was at the English Club. Here he was allowed to stay on one condition: that, as a Dutchman, he did not use the swimming pool.

Another 'leaf expert' who visited us was Ronnie Brown. He and I drove down from Addis Ababa to Dire Dawa without incident, although we had to skirt the notorious Danakil Desert. At Dire Dawa, apart from a few French, there were some American oilmen and British members of the Desert Locust Control Organisation. Life in the desert was harsh and lonely. In this African 'Wild West' town, the only diversions were hard drinking and whoring.

On the return journey with Brown, unusually it rained and the Land Rover slithered on the mushy, black cotton soil. It became darker and darker and we were some way from our destination at Awash Station. At dusk we came to a wide wadi in full spate but, despite this, Brown insisted that we attempt to ford it. The waters in the middle were well over the exhaust and we got stuck. The prospect of a night among the Danakil with their castration custom was, to say the least, unwelcome. After an hour another Land Rover miraculously appeared on the other side of the wadi and towed us out. We arrived at Awash at about midnight, tired but mightily relieved.

My job was to extend the distribution of the existing brand, while introducing a new low-priced brand, Gisilla. A. Besse & Co had trading warehouses in most of the main towns in Ethiopia so it was not difficult to get them to stock our products. Most of these warehouses were managed by African Greeks – that is Greeks born in Africa or half-castes, the Galla and Amharic Greeks. Some of them spoke a smattering of French, but none spoke English. All spoke Galla, Amharic and Arabic.

A. Besse bought produce and sold merchandise to Yemeni Arab wholesalers who sold on to retailers. Our policy – as elsewhere in the world – was to ensure that our brands were fresh (we took back stale cigarettes) and sold everywhere at the same price. We absorbed the freight costs to enable us to sell at the same price throughout Ethiopia, while ensuring also that the retail price remained competitive and that there was a constant level of supply.

With Ethiopian Airlines having an extensive fleet of Dakotas, it proved possible to avoid lengthy journeys and most cigarettes were delivered to depots by air. Those consignments of cigarettes delivered to depots by road required four-wheel track vehicles to navigate some of the worst surfaces in the world. A Land Rover could get lost in the worst potholes!

Negotiating and monitoring distribution arrangements – given the language barrier – was time-consuming and led to many misunderstandings. A year after I arrived, the Gisilla brand was introduced and the only promotional material to support this was a handbill with a picture of the packet which featured a leaping leopard and the price written in Amharic. To my surprise, the Greek

My parents on their wedding day

My family home in Rangoon

My father as Burma Golf Champion

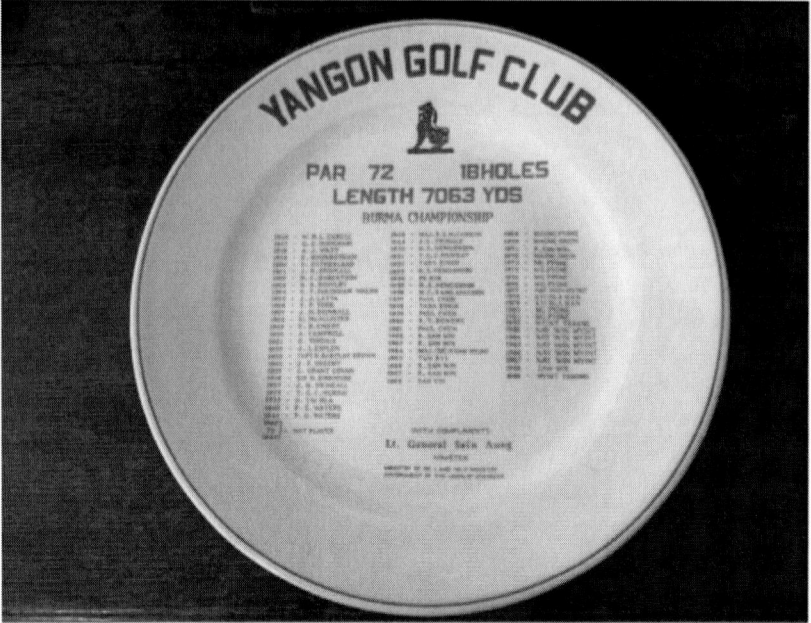

Both fathers on the same plate!

Colonial life in Burma

Coxing down under

2nd Lt Sheehy, back row left, eclipsed by bearskin

Second from L in second row: My sister in Moscow

Tobacco brothers – in Cuba with Fidel Castro

Uzbekistan: President Karimov on my L

Visiting a monastery in Ethiopia

manager in Gore suggested that few, if any, of the local Gallas could recognise a picture of a cigarette packet and certainly would not recognise a very life-sized picture of a leopard. Indeed, when we tested this among the crowds in the market, it proved to be the case. Nonetheless, the handbills were very popular – proving that the most effective advertising was 'word of mouth'.

Visiting one market in particular, in Gore, a sight was pointed out to me of a rather distinguished elderly Amhara riding a well-fed mule and accompanied by two assistants on foot who were collecting a handful of grain from each roadside stall. Apparently, when the rider had been a young man at the court of Emperor Menelik II he had been found guilty of stealing and had one hand cut off. Subsequently, his innocence was established and, as recompense, he was allowed to travel around the markets in Gore province taking one handful of produce from each stall. Over the years, the stalls had grown considerably and collecting grain had become a rewarding business.

I had always wanted to visit the tax-free enclave on Ethiopia's western border with the Sudan. We flew to Dembi Dollo where four of us transferred to a Jeep for the descent of the escarpment via a very rocky track. A puncture at about a third of the way into the journey meant we now had no spare tyre. Then, about half-way, there was another puncture – it would have been impossible to go with a flat tyre and we had no repair kit. Then the driver spotted I had sticking plaster on my hand. Using the roll of it in my luggage, we repaired the inner tube which lasted not only down to the enclave, but also all the way back to Dembi Dollo. Necessity is truly the mother of invention!

As well as travelling by road, I used to fly all over Ethiopia in Dakotas flown by American pilots from TWA which had the contract for Ethiopian Airlines. Sitting on a bench along the side of the fuselage, usually surrounded by a cargo of cigarettes and coffee, my fellow passengers were often chickens and goats. The 'airports' consisted of grass air strips and on one occasion, just after it had rained, we landed near Lake Tana in thick grass which concealed a bog. At the makeshift terminal, the pilot asked the agent why he had not lowered the flag to indicate it was too dangerous to land. He replied that the local Chief, who was desperate to hitch a lift on the plane to Addis, had threatened to shoot him if he did!

In eastern Nigeria they say: "All work and no play makes James a dull boy." In Addis Ababa, however, there was quite a lot of play. There were a number of foreign communities which largely kept to themselves. There was a smallish British community, led by the Ambassador who lived in the Embassy compound where most of his staff were housed. There were a couple of English girl clerks who were much in demand.

I became very friendly with the British Consul, Ronnie Peel, and his wife Diana who lived life to the full and were immensely hospitable. As well as dinner parties and casino evenings, Ronnie organised duck and game shooting expeditions. Other friends who joined in were Micky Brown, ex-Brigade of Guards, who was to die of a heart attack in his early forties. Micky worked for David Keown-Boyd, part owner of a trading house who was also a keen shot and most convivial companion.

Then there was Count Dickie Von Elst. None of us actually knew what Dickie did during the war. His family had owned vast estates in Silesia which were later confiscated by the Communists. He ran a small agency business, but I never discovered what merchandise he dealt in. But he was the most delightful man and he spoke every known European language and fluent Amharic, and was a remarkably good hunter and marksman. Needless to say, women were more than charmed by him. We remained friends until the mid-1990s when his failing eyesight caused us to lose touch.

Alongside the runway at the International Airport there was a nine-hole golf course. It was mostly used by the British and Americans. The American children were occasionally obstreperous in the one-room clubhouse. One day this led the First Secretary at the British Embassy, John Killick – later knighted and who became Ambassador in Moscow – to admonish a boy with the addendum: "God, how I hate American children! Especially those aged about thirty-five!"

In 1955 it was the twenty-fifth anniversary of Haile Selassie's coronation. Our house was on the processional route from the palace to the main church where the Jubilee was to be celebrated. I had a copy of Evelyn Waugh's 'A Coronation' from 1930 and, suffice to say, his description then was just as apt twenty five years on. Almost nothing had changed.

David Keown-Boyd had a cousin called Caroline Campbell who came to stay with him. She was a very beautiful girl who loved animals and the countryside. I fell madly in love with her. Although she only stayed a couple of weeks, we spent a lot of time together. After she left, I wangled some leave and visited her in England. She was the niece of Frank Packer – father of Kerry Packer. Frank invited us to the Savoy for dinner and dancing. At that time Frank was squiring a Dublin dress designer who was pretty and charming. It was a fun evening. Caroline remained the love of my life for the next two years.

Around the time of the Jubilee, the Emperor tried to emulate Royal Ascot by staging an Imperial Race Meeting. The main race would be the Imperial Ethiopian Gold Cup for horses bred from Ethiopian stock. Mike Martineau suggested we enter a horse. His friend, Wilson, had a marvellous-looking stallion which was too much of a handful for his wife, a keen horsewoman. We bought the horse but were soon aware how wild it was. Mike enjoyed galloping it and maintained it was very fast. We entered it for the Gold Cup under the name of Speedy Gonzalez after a Mexican sex maniac who was the main character in a well-known dirty story.

Just before the Gold Cup meeting, Sunny Bumper, a well-known horseman and jockey in Nairobi, arrived in Addis Ababa. He thought it would be an experience to take part in the inaugural race, but had no ride. At a party with our friends, the Peels, we described to Sunny what a magnificent horse Speedy was, with a fantastic turn of speed. He agreed to ride it out the following morning. His verdict: a nice-looking horse, but wild! There was no way he was going to risk his reputation riding Speedy in the race.

None of the Ethiopian jockeys could be enlisted to ride Speedy either. Mike Martineau was determined to race him and take the ride himself, if necessary. And that's what transpired, even though Mike was half as heavy again as any of the other jockeys.

Speedy looked magnificent in the paddock and attracted surprisingly good odds. On the way to the start, Speedy gave one of his rodeo displays but failed to unseat Mike. At the start, Speedy stood quietly. In fact, he was still standing there quietly but obstinately as the others finished. It was a shaming experience. Eventually, we gave Speedy back to the Wilsons.

On one of my sales tours, I travelled by road to Gondar in my VW Combi. I was as much interested in the journey itself as for the sales potential. I wanted to see Lake Tana – the source of the Nile. The Italian quarter of the city was on a hill on the outskirts of the Ethiopian area. The buildings had mostly been pillaged by the Ethiopians and goats and cattle sheltered in them. The floors were thick with earth and dung and it occurred to me that probably in centuries to come archaeologists would marvel at these remains of an Italian-African empire.

The hotel in which I stayed did not have dung on the bare floor, but the bedroom had no windows and there was a large hole in the ceiling. In the morning I was somewhat surprised to see someone wearing an Ampleforth Edwards House rugger shirt. I quickly recognised the voice - it was Tom Packenham. He was on an expedition which he described in his book 'The Mountains of Rasselas'. He had completed most of his journey, but welcomed the offer of a ride back to Addis Ababa. I was delighted to have an interesting and amusing companion, even if - at times - he did treat me as his 'dragoman'.

At Axum a French group were excavating a site which they had screened off and posted guards at the entrance. Tom embarrassed me by bursting past the guards on to the site and photographing it. He had letters of introduction to the governors of two provinces through which we were to pass. He dropped in at their palaces where he was comfortably housed and agreeably entertained. Of course, I was left to stay in the usual filthy hotels with their faeces-encrusted toilet seats. However, in his book he did include a picture of me ascending to a famous monastery, but with a slightly derogatory remark about my being 'hysterical with impatience' - a mood which my family will recognise as frequently occurring on our travels.

Another expedition, this time with David Keown-Boyd and Dickie Van der Elst, took place during the Christmas holidays of my last year in Ethiopia. The route was from Addis Ababa to Asmara, then on to Massawa, then across the Danakil Desert to Assab, and from there back to Addis Ababa. In Asmara, I visited one of my former salesmen who was anxious to show me his prize possessions. In his bedroom he opened his wardrobe and pulled out a Kalashnikov. No doubt he was a recruit in the guerrilla army that was preparing to free Eritrea from the Ethiopians. We spent Christmas and Boxing Day at Massawa, water skiing and fishing. The fishing was remarkable for the abundance of fish and we caught a huge amount. It was all great fun.

We estimated that it would take three days to cross the Danakil Desert, but just in case it took longer we asked some Italian friends in Assab to arrange for a search party to come looking for us on the fourth day.

Apart from the Danakil, the only people who inhabited the desert were the odd party of Desert Locust patrolmen. The tracks that their Land Rovers made were the only roads and as long as they were going east, we followed them in our Land Rovers. But every now and then the eastward track was obliterated by a large dune of sand – sometimes up to forty feet high – which had been blown there. Finding our way around these was not only time-consuming, but also used a lot of petrol.

After two days we were running short of petrol and water and our guide had lost our confidence. However, that evening in the distance we sighted an encampment which turned out to be a refuelling site for the Desert Locust patrol. Of course, it also had a well. They generously supplied us with fuel and water, but warned us that instead of being one day from Assab, it would take a minimum of three days – but we decided to go on. Apart from some scrubby desert near Assab, the track passed through a landscape that appeared to be littered with millions of cannonballs, which were volcanic rocks.

We were constantly on the lookout for the Danakil – as nomads, they were always on the move. Not knowing where their rival tribes were, they would send out a woman to reconnoitre the route ahead, for females were highly prized, unlike the men whom they would kill for their testicles. Should the woman not return by dusk, they knew where the rival tribe was. War then ensued. With so little grazing and almost no water wells along the barren route, we did not actually see any Danakils. On the fifth day, just as we were nearing Assab, whom did we meet but our search party which had promised to set out on the fourth day!

I got back to Addis Ababa two or three days late. Don Hunt had not been the least bit perturbed about my whereabouts, although some of my colleagues had begun to worry. I had started to think that I was condemned to remain in Ethiopia forever. I'd even seriously begun learning Amharic although I had more than a smattering of 'market' Amharic and Arabic. I was delighted, therefore, when Hunt told me I was to be transferred to Jamaica.

Chapter Eight

I spent most of my home leave in 1957 wooing Caroline Campbell. I stayed two weekends with her and her parents at their home in Beaulieu in Hampshire. Caroline's mother was Australian and her father was an Anglicised taciturn Scot. I got the distinct impression that they had someone a bit more aristocratic in mind for Caroline – if not with a title, then at least with a substantial estate.

However, I was not deterred and Caroline was as adorable as ever: but to no avail. I was devastated when she told me that she would not marry me. After that meeting I never saw her again, but some five or six years later she wrote to me saying she had seen me driving through East Grinstead. She urged me to meet her but I did not reply.

I also saw a lot of my great friend Michael Bonfield, who was still working for ICI in Cheshire and who, by now, was heavily involved with his future wife. We played a certain amount of golf on championship courses in the north, such as Hoylake, Birkdale and Lytham, and took a week's tour of Scotland playing Troon, Gullane and Muirfield. Our friendship deepened and to me Michael had become a brother to all intents and purposes.

During this time my mother lived in a flat in Latymer Court in Hammersmith. My sister Ann also had a flat there. My mother's flat was small with only one bathroom. She was largely overwhelmed by my presence, but particularly underwhelmed one day when I spent so long in the bath reading a newspaper that she had to go to Hammersmith Tube station to use the loo. On reflection, I did abuse her hospitality.

My other sister, Mary, had left university and gone to Canada to work for the Canadian Broadcasting Service. Mary was sharing a flat with another Cambridge graduate who was also working for CBS. It is extraordinary to recall that when she went up to Cambridge she had a medical and she was diagnosed with tuberculosis. In those days, her treatment consisted of being bedridden in a TB clinic for almost a year, after which she resumed her studies.

As a child, I had enjoyed my sea voyages to and from Australia and had long wanted to travel on a transatlantic liner to North America. So I arranged a trip on a Holland America liner to visit Mary in Toronto and then fly down to Jamaica and my new posting.

The voyage across the Atlantic was dull – there was not enough time to get to know anybody. Toronto was dull, too. At that time it was quite a small city with its buildings crammed together along the lakeside. It had wide, straight streets that seemed to go all the way to Vancouver! It was still very much a Scots Presbyterian community: alcohol could only be bought at a government liquor store and, even in summer, you were not allowed to drink alcohol in your garden or, indeed, anywhere in the open. Noel Coward is alleged to have aptly summed up Toronto by saying: "Now I understand why there was a shortage of servants in Scotland."

I was not attracted to Canada and was glad to be on my way to Jamaica. Before landing at Kingston, the plane stopped at Montego Bay where we were greeted by a calypso band and free rum punches. After Abyssinia, I thought that this was the life for me although the rum punch tasted foul and had a frightful smell. In my four years in the Caribbean, I never drank rum again. While I quite got to like calypsos, steel bands bore me.

On arriving in Kingston I was taken to a small hotel, the Flamingo, where it was planned that I should stay until I found myself accommodation. BAT did not own accommodation for its expatriate staff in the western hemisphere. After two weeks at the Flamingo, I became a member of the Liguanea Club where there were guestrooms, a swimming pool and a nine-hole golf course. I moved in there.

The BAT company in Jamaica was B & J .B. Machado, which was originally a cigar producer. It now produced cigars in one factory and cigarettes in another, both on the same site. The cigars were hand-rolled and all for export – mainly, if not exclusively, for the UK. It was a troubled operation and shortly after my arrival it merged with another cigar manufacturer who was more capable of dealing with the truculent, and sometimes violent, knife-wielding cigar workers. In their work these men use very sharp knives to shape the leaves before rolling.

My role was to take over from Tony Player as sales manager (BAT had not yet discovered marketing). The general manager was Tommy Thompson who had risen from the ranks to become an officer in the Army, and had risen from the shop floor to become manager at BAT's Liverpool factory. But with no business education he was out of his managerial depth and was particularly inept at negotiations with Michael Manley, the chief negotiator and secretary of the left-wing National Workers Union. Michael was the son of Norman Washington Manley, the island's Prime Minister and leader of the left-wing People's National Party. Labour was the right-wing party led by the charismatic Alexander Bustamante.

Michael Manley had been educated in England where he attended the London School of Economics – thus gaining impeccable socialist credentials. He was very articulate and picked up his negotiating skills from his father, a successful barrister. Michael ran rings around Tommy in negotiations which mostly resulted in victories for the workers. Tommy worried obsessively about the negotiations and consoled himself by drinking too much.

The company's finance manager was Arthur Sudbury, a fastidious man who was very punctilious: he arrived at work on the dot; took his lunch for precisely the amount of time allowed; and never worked a moment late in the evening. He never travelled outside Kingston, rarely entertained and when you did get to visit his house you were not allowed to walk on the white carpet in the drawing room.

The chief accountant, a Jamaican called Mr Taylor, was very hard-working, conscientious and a committed company man. A high officer in the Masonic movement, he paid me the compliment of inviting me to join the local lodge. As a Catholic, I declined.

There was a small leaf department at May Pen between Kingston and Mandeville run by Douglas Kyle, assisted by Greville Stone. They kept very much to themselves, rarely visiting Kingston. The Virginia flue-cured leaf they produced was almost unsmokeable as was the air-cured cigarette tobacco. This was Machado's problem.

The most colourful character in the company was a Bajan, Campbell Yarwood. Unattractive to look at with a ruddy complexion and projecting, uneven teeth, he wore shapeless, scruffy clothes with his shirt out most of the time. But Campbell had an attractive personality. He was interested in everyone and everything. He had definite views, most expressed in amusing and colourful language with a West Indian flavour and accent. He was particularly fond of cricket, horse racing and rum. But, above all, he loved his delightful wife Irma and his children. Campbell was generous to a fault and many were the hours of an evening I spent carousing on his veranda.

While in Jamaica we had three or four assistants. Two I remember were the worthy Jimmy Spiers and a rather pushy Yorkshireman called Geoff Hardwick. Hardwick's wife, Maureen, scandalised the rather prissy expatriate community by taking a job singing in a rather seedy nightclub. Nevertheless, after serving as Managing Director in Bangladesh for BAT, Hardwick went on to become a moderately-successful property developer on Tobago.

During the Second World War and up to the mid-sixties, BAT's Central America and Caribbean companies had been run from Louisville, Kentucky. But BAT wanted to centralise management at Millbank and to introduce a more contemporary management approach. Machado was considered to be a company in need of this treatment, especially as they were expecting competition from imported Craven A cigarettes produced by Carreras. So it was decided to strengthen the sales team by sending myself and Mike Majoram to Machado. Mike was a fastidious character with a good sense of humour. He stayed in the flat which I rented: he still thinks I charged him too much for his room!

The real problem turned out to be not only that new sales management was needed in Jamaica but that new directors were also needed in London.

With Jamaican smokers wanting quality filter cigarettes, Machado's requested permission to buy filter tip machinery, only to be told by London that BAT worldwide had a huge interest in non-filter cigarettes and so they should encourage smokers to buy plain cigarettes – it's what the company wanted.

As far as plain cigarettes were concerned, there was a further problem. Machado's had given an undertaking to the Jamaican government to replace cigarette leaf imports with locally-grown leaf. Unfortunately, the smoking quality of the local leaf was atrocious. There was almost a direct correlation between the percentage of local leaf substitution and Machado's decline in market share.

In the autumn of 1957, to introduce its more modern management philosophy throughout Latin America and the Caribbean, BAT summoned the senior regional management to a conference at French Lick in Indiana [USA]- renowned for being the home of Pluto Water, a mild laxative, which we were to discover came out of the hotel taps.

Mike and I decided that on the way to French Lick, we would stop off at

Havana. We arrived after dark to find a deserted and rather sinister Cuban city with Ford Falcons touring the streets, reputedly with trigger happy plain-clothes police inside them.

Things improved when we got to the hotel district along the Malecon which was brightly lit and alive with American tourists. Although Fidel Castro was still in the mountains in eastern Cuba, his guerrillas were operating almost at will throughout the country. To all intents and purposes, Havana was under siege.

We stayed at the Riviera Hotel – which is still there – then owned by George Raft and the Mafia establishment. The ground floor was a casino and gambling went on twenty-four hours a day, seven days a week. Above the bar there was a combo playing Latin music. We lingered for a while in the casino before going to bed.

The next day we hired a taxi for a tour of Havana. The contrast between the abject poverty of Old Havana and the remarkable affluence of the Miramar area was startling and, in itself, was surely justification for Castro's revolutionary activities. Well into our taxi tour we passed an imposing building which our driver informed us was the new library with, as yet, no books. This stood next to the university which had no students (it had been closed). The next grand building was the Palais de Justice – "but there is no justice," commented the driver.

That evening we went to the Tropicana nightclub where there was a big band extravaganza in the Busby Berkeley idiom – lots of gorgeous girls everywhere, most memorably up in the trees. This was quite something after the tawdry nightlife of Jamaica. There were very few tourist hotels in Cuba. Most American tourists left Florida in the evening and then drank, danced, gambled and fornicated all night, before returning to Miami around midday.

On arrival at the French Lick Hotel in Indiana, we were greeted by one or two people who appeared to be there to help us. I asked one of them to carry my bags to Reception. Unfortunately, it was E.M. Bruton, the Deputy Chairman! Most of the delegates were American – tobacco farmers from Georgia and the Carolinas. They were earthy, hard-drinking, chain-smoking men with a self-taught knowledge of growing and processing tobacco. Few had any comprehension of marketing or distribution and probably none could read a profit-and-loss statement or a balance sheet. This financial illiteracy was prevalent throughout BAT including, I suspect, many main board directors.

The content of this conference had been put together by Desmond Misselbrook, whom I had first met when he interviewed me on my application to join the company after leaving the Army. The lectures were listened to politely with few questions; most of the delegates reckoned they were too old to change. Anyway, things were going OK in their companies, so why was change needed? Furthermore, they had not seen many of their colleagues for some time and were far more preoccupied in 'chewing the fat' with old friends.

Later, I heard that Misselbrook was not altogether surprised that the conference had failed to re-educate BAT's management in Latin America. He believed that changing BAT was a ten to fifteen-year process. You first had to recruit and then train new, young managers and only when they had succeeded to key jobs would BAT's management style be contemporary and competitive. He was right.

When Mike Majoram and I returned to Jamaica, we explained the content of the conference to Tommy and Arthur, who derided it amid much hilarity. From a business point of view, most of my three years in Jamaica was frustrating. Marketing and distributing plain cigarettes that were inevitably declining in demand was hardly motivating. Towards the end of my stay we started importing Matinee Filter Tip which targeted women smokers and had a limited appeal to male cane cutters.

Visiting the tourist hotels on the north coast and chatting up the single girls holidaying there was an expensive diversion. But most of one's diversions were in Kingston. I became a member of the Constant Springs Golf Club, one of the oldest courses on the island and played there a lot. Most of my weekends were spent at Constant Springs. After golf, there was a lot of drinking which invariably ended up in a lot of singing. I made many good friends there, one of whom was Bob Cardy, a Unilever export manager.

Bob had been a glider pilot in the war and had taken part in the Sicily and Arnhem operations. To say he glided into Sicily was a slight exaggeration as the American plane towing him slipped a tow rope early and Bob's team ended up in the sea. Clinging to the wreckage, one of Bob's Cockney comrades remarked: "If the missus could see me now, I bet she'd be dusting off the insurance policy on the mantelpiece." A fountain of earthy humour, Bob was the heaviest smoker I've ever met – one who could roll the cigarette with his lips from side to side of his mouth. He finally quit at the age of 90 but continued to be the life and soul of his local British Legion and a perennial visitor to Arnhem.

After a year, I went on leave to the UK during which time I met my future wife Jill. We saw a great deal of each other – particularly in Winston's nightclub on Bond Street, to which I was addicted. At that time, the resident cabaret was Danny la Rue and Ronnie Corbett. Our romance blossomed and we agreed that we should marry on my next leave in eighteen months' time, but that we should not announce our engagement just yet.

On my return to Jamaica I gradually found myself becoming enchanted by Alison, the wife of Ferdy, a golfing friend. They had been married for a few years, but with no children. Ferdy was a really decent fellow: not very bright but good company. Alison, however, was very, very bright, a successful eye specialist and very pretty to boot.

I betrayed Jill by falling madly in love with Alison. It was an anguished love. As a Catholic, it was morally wrong of me to fall in love with another man's wife. Where was it leading to? Marriage? I confessed my betrayal to Jill, which devastated her. Jill's mother, with every justification, never forgave me.

My affair with Alison grew in intensity. Neither of us wanted it to end, but neither of us could decide how it should go on. Eventually, I was transferred to Barbados and we decided it was best to end things. However, Alison did visit me once in Barbados and we realised we were still madly in love. Even so, when she returned to Jamaica, that really was the end of it.

Chapter Nine

I had enjoyed life in Jamaica. But, as far as business was concerned, I felt I had not achieved very much. Now I was off to Barbados. At twenty-nine, to be the manager of a self-contained subsidiary company on an island 9,000 miles from head office was a great opportunity, even if it wasn't especially challenging. BAT Barbados had ninety-five per cent of the market, with the other five per cent held by Benson & Hedges and du Maurier, both 'incognito' BAT imported brands.

Although there remained a British Governor in Barbados, by 1960 it had become self-governing and the Prime Minister was Sir Grantley Adams. In contrast to Jamaica where latent class and racial tensions had been fanned by Michael Manley and the Rastas, Barbados was a tolerant and happy society.

Barbados was the only Caribbean island that had always been British, who had claimed it in 1625. Its main wealth derived from sugar, which had relied upon slave labour until emancipation. The British had decreed that for every 100 slaves, a plantation needed ten white men. The cheapest means of employing white men was by purchasing indentured labour: these men were criminals who had avoided prison by being sent abroad to work on plantations.

Unlike a slave, who was always a slave and could be bought or sold, many being quite valuable, indentured labourers were a depreciating asset as they were tied for a fixed term which the plantation paid for. After that, they were free. As a consequence, the plantation owners often treated his white indentured labour no better, and sometimes worse, than his more valuable tradable slaves.

The Barbados blacks, while resenting the white slave owners, had no complexes about the white indentured labour. As most of the whites in Barbados were descended from them, in contrast to Jamaica neither colour nor class was a problem. Another factor in the happy disposition of Barbadians was the seamless British connection. In all the other islands, the Spanish, French, Indian and Chinese had miscegenated with the blacks which had resulted in fiery temperaments. Barbadian blacks had interbred with phlegmatic white Anglo-Saxons.

It was unlikely that there would be another opportunity in my lifetime to be paid to live and work in such a delightful island setting and I was determined to make the most of it. I moved into a bungalow on Bluewater Beach and six months later switched to a flat on the beach at St Lawrence. I had a trusty, cheerful and discreet maid called Pilgrim.

The company employed about 100 people. There was a factory with primary, making and packing departments. Machinery was antique with old cutters in the primary department with locally-made cylinder dryers. In the making department, we had Molins' Mark Fives producing 500 cigarettes a minute compared to the 3,000 a minute used by most of the industry. In the packing department, we had two ten shell-and-slide machines, while incredibly we made twenties cup packings by hand. The total output was ten million to fifteen million cigarettes a month.

The factory manager was Rogers, a white from a poor family. His Bajan was so pronounced it was difficult to understand. In his youth he had been an outstanding cricketer and been selected to play for Barbados against Jamaica. However, his boss at BAT refused to release him and, as he needed the job, he never got another invitation.

When I started, I had to endure a two to three-week handover from the previous manager, Brian Burgess-Webb. I say 'endured' because Brian was cocky and recounted his preposterous experiences with complete conviction. He claimed he had ridden in the Grand National, fallen off his horse, remounted and finished third. Nobody took Brian seriously and he left the company and the island unloved.

There were two white accountants – Keith Piggott and Tony Stoute. They were very efficient and very helpful. Marketing and distribution was managed by David Weatherall.

I had a splendid Bajan chauffeur called Shepherd. Cricket captains are called 'skippers' and that is what he called me. He had a great turn of phrase and once, during a discussion about a cricketer, he described him as a 'black man'. "Blacker than you Shepherd?" I enquired. "Oh yes," came the reply. "Him so black that he could go to a funeral naked!"

My job occupied me about two to three hours a day and on some days there was even less work to do. Every morning before breakfast, I swam in the sea – it was invigorating. As one of my Bajan friends remarked as he emerged from the waves: "After that, I feel like a new woman!"

Each afternoon and evening I played golf, mostly at Bluewater, but occasionally at Sandy Lane, which had recently been developed and was owned by Ronald Tree. When I arrived in Barbados he had just completed a nine-hole golf course. To obtain a licence, the club had to have committee members resident on the island. Tree did not encourage Bajans to be members as he wanted it exclusively for rich tourists and his wealthy friends who had properties nearby. So, as a non-Bajan resident, I was invited to join the inaugural committee.

There were two great characters in Barbados at that time: 'Poppa' Daish and Jack Egan. Both had lived on the island for many years and were regarded as Bajan. They liked gambling and drinking, especially Egan. So much so that Jack was officially warned by his doctor about his habit, to which he replied: "My observations over a long life is that I have seen far more old drunks than I have seen old doctors!" Once a week Poppa and Jack would host a lunch in a ramshackle hunting cabin in marshland close to the airport, to which I was occasionally invited. Some poker was played with plenty of drinking and chat. The stories they used to tell are memorable but unprintable!

After my love affair with Alison had ended, I consoled myself with an affair with a rather jolly Barbadian girl but it was never going anywhere. I had hoped to stay in Barbados for eighteen months, but after ten months there were suggestions that I should go to Canada and join Imperial Tobacco, the BAT associate there. One way and another, the company wanted me out because they needed my job for a shortly-to-be-retiring West Indian factory manager with seven children whom they did not have the heart to make redundant.

Chapter Ten

In the event, I didn't go to Canada, but was sent on leave early and told I would be joining a new operational team in London. The Marketing Advisory Service [MAS] had been up and running for a year when I joined it in 1962. Two years earlier, BAT had become alarmed at the rapid growth of Rothmans worldwide. Anton Rupert, an academic and engineer by trade, had seen how badly BAT's South African subsidiary, United Tobacco, had been run. His Rembrandt Tobacco Company bought Rothmans, a small UK company, in 1954 and Carreras four years later, more for their brands than their existing volumes.

In South Africa, Rothmans had already severely damaged BAT's business where Rupert had introduced American-style cigarettes and, at that time, the 'pseudo international' brands such as Rothmans King Size Filter [1957] and Peter Stuyvesant [1954], correctly calculating that US-blend style cigarettes would be attractive to the blacks, while the international Virginia filter brands would appeal to the whites. Meanwhile, BAT followed with poor imitations, both in brand presentation and the quality of the blends – that is, the smoking quality.

Rupert used the proceeds from his success in South Africa – BAT's share there had declined from one hundred per cent to thirty per cent – to buy cigarette companies in Germany, Holland, Belgium, Switzerland, Australia and New Zealand. He also announced plans to establish companies in Malaya, Singapore and Northern and Southern Rhodesia. In all these countries, BAT had a substantial, often total, market share. By 1962, it was clear that the formula of international king size brands of good smoking quality together with more modern presentations of local filter brands was making dramatic inroads into BAT's business.

One of the secrets of Rupert's success was his strategy of encouraging prominent local businessmen to participate in his operations as significant shareholders. These shareholders could then influence policy at government level. BAT did issue shares in its overseas subsidiaries on local markets but not selectively, thereby missing a trick.

Rupert had also identified that the Duty-free business was one of huge potential which, apart from its profitability, would make the international brands truly global. The threat to BAT's Duty-free business was a threat to its most profitable business line, because it was the company's only UK cash generator. The rest of its income was mainly dividends from overseas subsidiaries. The main reason that BAT's exports from the UK were so profitable was the Duty Drawback that the exports enjoyed.

It was the Ardath Cigarette Company in the 1920s that discovered this loophole. BAT could not understand how Ardath export cigarettes were so much more profitable than its own, but in 1925 they bought the company and found out. Ardath was the begetter of State Express family of brands – 333, 666, 777 and 999. State Express, being a well-known US train, was the main rival in the Far East against Rothmans King Size. The other was Benson & Hedges brand [B&H] to which BAT had bought the worldwide trademark excluding the Americas. BAT was very content with B&H as a discreet subsidiary with its own marketing. It was this 'smart' subsidiary that developed B&H King Size in its unique gold-foil, hinge-lid pack. They also distributed du Maurier.

BAT's Australian associate, Amatil, with its tobacco subsidiary, WD & HO Wills, was the first company to wake up to the dire threat from Rothmans and the board in London allowed them to market B&H Golden Boy as an international brand to compete against Rothmans King Size.

The market share of WD & HO Wills New Zealand in 1962 had avalanched from one hundred per cent to thirty per cent and was still falling. It was to this company that the MAS team, of which I was a member, was sent. The team was led by a main board director, John Husbands, and also included Leslie Craigan.

John Husbands was an extraordinary man. He left school at fifteen and sometime later went to America, joined the BAT subsidiary Brown & Williamson, and was sent to work in Latin America. In Nicaragua he married a local girl, but his real achievement was building the business in Venezuela. Under his leadership, he got the local subsidiary to take over eighty per cent of market share, which it still holds today. John was also an entrepreneur in his own right. In Venezuela, he was a partner in a nightclub in Caracas, while in the UK he ran a large and successful poultry business near East Grinstead. He was a workaholic with a penchant for parties and women.

Leslie Craigan was from Northern Ireland and a clever, articulate extrovert who was enjoyable company. Leslie had joined BAT sometime after me and had worked mostly in Nigeria. Having spent our careers in Africa, Leslie and I were excited about going to New Zealand via America. We were keen as mustard to do a good job and eager to find out as much as we could about the country and the company.

Our enthusiasm was soon blunted. We were met by BAT's sixty-year-old sales manager when we arrived in the early morning at Auckland. He was to drive us on the day-long trip to Wellington. As soon as we were in the car, he told us that he was a nervous driver and that he would appreciate it if we did not talk about the company during the journey. That silent drive was a prelude to the strained atmosphere throughout our visit. About this time, and following a trip to Australia, Clement Freud was asked in a TV interview whether he had visited New Zealand. "No, because I'm told it is closed," he replied.

Indeed, trade unions – including farmers' cooperatives – and a feeling of 'welfare statism' had virtually shut off all competitiveness and entrepreneurship. Opening hours for shops and other service establishments were limited. Pubs closed at 6pm, hotels even discouraged guests at weekends by charging exorbitant supplements. Working hours were fixed and overtime minimal. Price controls and exchange controls were in force and levels of taxation were very high. The brightest New Zealanders were all leaving the country.

This culture had permeated the company. Complacency was prevalent and the attitude to the MAS team seemed to be: "Those Poms in MAS do not understand our business and, anyway, they are not welcome." It made us all the more determined to introduce reality.

The programme we worked to had four stages. The first was 'Product Quality and Competitive Analysis'. Depending on the number of products on the market, we spent two or three days assessing the quality of our products with rival brands. This included presentation, packing and a subjective assessment of smoking quality.

The second was 'Market Familiarisation'. We spent a week to ten days visiting wholesalers and retailers and talking to consumers and advertising and market research agencies.

Thirdly, there were 'Strategic and Tactical Recommendations'. On returning to head office we reviewed the marketing and distribution strategies, after which we reached the final stage and wrote our 'Report' with our findings and recommendations. We presented our report to the local board and the main BAT board director in London responsible for New Zealand.

We had been appalled by what we had found: it was hardly surprising that the company was in such dire straits. But, as was usually the case, it was not the fault of the people in the front line; rather, it was the management in the boardroom.

The general manager was an introverted, secretive Englishman who came from a factory management background with no commercial sense. He did not like Kiwis and they did not like him. He and his sales and marketing director rarely spoke. There was no strategic or operational leadership.

Presenting our report to the New Zealand board was largely a waste of time. The only good that came from the report was that Leslie Craigan was transferred there to help them sort out the mess. It was a Herculean task, particularly as Rothmans were very active and very effective.

Travelling with the MAS teams over four years, operating with the same procedures everywhere we went, became the pattern of my life. The countries visited were: Nigeria, Ghana, Syria, Liberia, the Congo, Southern and Northern Rhodesia, South Africa, Mauritius, Kenya, Uganda, Tanzania, Lebanon, Iraq, Kuwait, Bahrain, Saudi Arabia, Spain, Portugal, France, Italy, Holland, Belgium, Denmark, Norway, Finland, Sweden, Switzerland, Pakistan, Bangladesh, Ceylon [now Sri Lanka], Hong Kong, Argentina, Chile, Brazil, Venezuela, Costa Rica, Panama, Nicaragua, Jamaica, Trinidad and Canada.

Some memories of these visits stand out, particularly in Ghana and the Congo. In Ghana, the country was suffering from the legacy of Nkrumah's profligacy. The economy was disintegrating and so was the company's business. The Pioneer Tobacco Company had developed a very successful leaf tobacco scheme. Similar to schemes in other countries, BAT did not own or lease any agricultural land in Ghana. Small farmers were contracted to grow and cure leaf for the company. Initially, they bought seedlings from the company, progressing rapidly to growing their own.

The company arranged credit for farmers to buy farming implements, fertilisers and materials to build curing barns. Most importantly, BAT supplied a free extension service which advised on how to grow and cure quality tobacco. Farmers under contract to the company grew as little as a quarter of an acre of tobacco, compared to large farms which might grow two to three acres. By 1961 the scheme was producing sixty per cent of Pioneer's tobacco requirements. But the government's socialist advisers did not approve of the capitalist-entrepreneurial nature of the scheme. The farmers were making too much money which party officials believed they should share. Fairness had to prevail and what could be fairer than cooperatives?

It was decreed that farmers were forbidden to cure their own tobacco. They had to sell the green leaf to co-op curing stations where a standard price per pound would be paid. Of course, the price paid was far lower than the company paid and there was little incentive for the farmer to produce quality tobacco. The result was that volume collapsed and what was produced was pretty unsmokeable. So Ghana, a country strapped for foreign exchange, had to import tobacco to sustain its revenue from taxes on cigarettes.

When politicians and others call for 'fairness', it invariably means levelling down rather than up. Because of the chaotic state of tobacco supply, our visit to Ghana was frustrating.

In 1962 I was sent on a one-man mission to the Congo. Mobutu had just taken over and the Belgians had fled, literally. All whites were assumed to be Belgians and were, thus, under suspicion, threats and disapproval. It was a sorry situation. Our manager there, a Frenchman called Mike Premet, had been transferred from Saigon, another hotspot at that time. He and his wife were very calm and reassuring. Not so his marketing manager, a Belgian called Louis Balyou. The Congolese did not like Louis' manner and he had to leave the country in a hurry. He and his wife were glad to go. Eventually, he became BAT's agent in Reunion and retired a very rich man.

Before the Belgian debacle, BAT's factory had been in Stanleyville; a makeshift plant had also been established in a warehouse in Leopoldville. My job was to survey the markets in and around Leopoldville, where most of the money was, and in and around Stanleyville, where most of our market share used to exist.

On journeys around Leopoldville, and to and from Matadi, I was comfortable as long as I had a Congolese salesman and a driver with me. But on one occasion I had to fly to Stanleyville on my own. Half way there the plane had to stop at a self-proclaimed republic which was emulating Katanga under Tshombe. All passengers had to disembark and show their passports and health certificates. As far as this new republic was concerned, my typhoid and paratyphoid vaccinations were out of date. I had to pay an exorbitant sum to be re-vaccinated with an old razor blade scratching my arm and a white liquid being applied. As soon as I got back on the plane, I rushed to the toilet and vigorously washed it all off.

It was evening when the plane eventually arrived at Stanleyville. The airport was deserted and dirty and the surly staff unwelcoming. The BAT manager met me and drove me to the hotel which was also deserted and dirty. The European and commercial quarter of Stanleyville was deserted. There was a Barclays Bank manager and two or three other expatriates, plus a few Greek traders and missionaries. But, otherwise, it was a ghost town. The management class had legged it.

Although most of the Belgian expatriates had fled, it was important not to abandon the factory. On visiting it the following day, I found a sorry sight. Few machines were working. With a lack of leaf and wrapping materials, plus a lack of mechanical skills, production was only ten per cent of capacity. None of the Congolese workers had been laid off and the place was teeming with them, most standing around and wondering what was happening.

I greatly admired BAT's manager, a former mechanic from Liverpool who had accepted the task of trying to maintain some manufacturing in Stanleyville. Despite not speaking a word of Lingala or French, he was busy organising the production, including helping to keep the machinery going.

The next day, accompanied by a Congolese sales rep and a driver, I visited markets around Stanleyville. It was an uncomfortable experience. At village after village there were roadblocks manned by scruffily-uniformed militia armed with Kalashnikovs and red-eyed with drink. Fortunately, bribed with sufficient quantities of cigarettes, they allowed us to pass.

Distribution of our products in the markets I visited was non-existent. Rather incongruously at this time, our main brand in the Congo was Militaire, whose packets pictured soldiers marching through the jungle behind the Belgian flag. The return journey to Leopoldville was uneventful and from there I flew to Nairobi.

East Africa – that is, Kenya, Uganda and Tanzania – were contemplating becoming a federation. In many ways they were already a loose federation, but this was before independence. Elected leaders wanted to become 'kings of their own castles' and very much went their own way.

Our visit was very routine. My task was to survey the market in Tanzania. My main memory of this trip was of a late-night drinking session with one or two of the marketing staff, one of whom was aptly named Murdo Christie. He was a tall, well-built Scot, pleasant enough when he was sober, but who got more and more aggressive with drink. As his level of alcohol rose, his facial expression became quite manic. It was terrifying. Murdo was eventually transferred to British Guiana as the general manager.

This job proved too much for him and he became insane. The problem was how to remove him without certifying him. Another GM was sent out to British Guiana and had to operate from a hotel, visiting the office every evening after Murdo had gone and cancelling all the irrational decisions he had made during the day. Eventually, he was persuaded to take some home leave and after a period of treatment, a psychiatrist declared him fully recovered. I was asked to take him on my MAS team, but was not convinced of his sanity. A few months later he murdered his wife in front of her mother in the kitchen of their home after breakfast.

We had a similar experience with that same psychiatrist when we sent home a colleague from the Sudan who was unstable. The psychiatrist's verdict was that the man was sane and perhaps it was his management that needed attention. Psychiatry, some say, is the study of those who don't need it by those who do. I tend to concur.

One of my colleagues in the MAS was a large, extrovert Welshman called David Jenkins who had worked most of his time in Malaysia and Singapore. David was an enthusiast, but not very bright. When he was late one morning for an appointment in Finland, he confessed to me some time afterwards it was because he had propositioned a chambermaid, who had succumbed to his charm and his wallet. Our David was quite a normal, healthy sex maniac, but I cautioned him that the average man only had 5,000 "shots in the locker". "Really?" said David, who immediately started calculating his current strike rate. "Good Lord," he added. "I only have 57 left!" Unfortunately, David became an alcoholic, went to live in Spain where booze was cheap, and died a lonely death.

In Northern Rhodesia we were invited to drinks and lunch at the Police Officers' Club where, somewhat seditiously, the *Gents* was titled 'John's Stone

House' and the *Ladies*, 'Barbara's Castle' – both were ministers for the colonies in the Labour government at the time.

On a trip to Venezuela, the former stomping ground of our director John Husbands, we decided we would trick him into providing us with a free evening of wine, women and song. With the help of the long-time manager of our local company C.A. Cigarerra Bigott, I located a nightclub John had once owned. We tried to take him there, but he refused to go in and was not at all amused.

It was on a trip to Saudi Arabia that I first met Wahib Bin Zagga, the son of our agent. Wahib had been educated in England and was very *évolué* for a Saudi in the mid-1960s. Jeddah was a scruffy port with very few modern buildings or roads and where development was just starting. Wahib, who was not married then, had deserted the family home for a small house under a flyover. There we used to chat long into the night, drinking champagne and whisky while he smoked his hookah. Wahib later married Dina, a Russian refugee from Soviet terror.

Nobleza was the name of BAT's Argentine company and it was not inappropriate. It was managed almost exclusively by Anglo-Argentines who believed themselves to be superior to the Latin-Argentines and the BAT management in London. They did not take kindly to the criticisms of their business and particularly to mine. Unfortunately, there were two Argentine directors on the main board who supported them, to my detriment.

MAS had been brought into being because worldwide BAT was complacent, inefficient and uncompetitive. It was inevitable that, if it was to be effective, it needed to shake up the subsidiary companies. Management did not like it, and many directors were uncomfortable because it reflected on their poor stewardship. The territorial directors were troubled by the MAS revelations undermining confidence and lowering morale. So inevitably it was decided that the MAS team had had their day.

Perhaps the final straw was an exposé I gave on international brands to a senior management course at the company's training establishment at Chelwood in Sussex. This showed that the phenomenal demand for international brands – such as Rothmans, Peter Stuyvesant, Dunhill and the Marlboro family – were in the ascendancy, compared with the declining market share of the BAT portfolio – such as B&H, State Express 555 and Lucky Strike. The delegates were depressed and appalled by the BAT position.

The session was attended by an Anglo-Argentine director, Hobson, who heard a chorus of concern from the delegates. Hobson reported back to the board and two days later I was severely reprimanded by the board for being alarmist: BAT's strengths, I should have emphasised, were its local brands. It was somewhat similar to the mind-set I had come up against in Jamaica where BAT's 'we are not filter cigarette specialists' attitude allowed our consumers to switch to international tipped brands owned by our competitors.

Richard Dobson was Deputy Chairman with responsibility for tobacco operations, although financing was the responsibility of the Chairman, Denzil Clarke. Dobson decided that MAS was damaging to morale and undermined the role of many of his territorial directors and so he decided to close us down. Fortunately, my director, John Husbands, still had two portfolios, tobacco businesses in Africa and with Geoffrey Rawlinson, another BAT director and Desmond Misselbrook, the Deputy Chairman, was responsible for the diversification strategy to reduce dependency on tobacco earnings. He appointed me his No.2, or Personal Assistant, as the title was then.

Two incidents concerning tobacco in West Africa stand out from that time. The first was a visit to Ghana. Having started my career there, I have always had great affection for Ghanaians and Ghana. I had known a prosperous and self-confident nation clamouring for independence. Now, thanks to Nkrumah, the country was pitifully broke. Prices were astronomically high: bread, I recall, was the equivalent of one pound a loaf. There was no money for spare parts: the 'mammy wagons' were literally running on tyres where you could see the inner tube.

As far as our factory was concerned, we had imported tobacco under a US-aid programme – cigarette tax was a highly important tax source, after all. But there were no medicines. They could not even import a football.

When I called in at the Presidential Palace in the Aburi Hills, I noticed that the guttering had rusty holes which had left orange streaks on the whitewashed walls. Inside, the carpets were filthy with the curtains hanging precariously and haphazardly from the railings. The President asked me if I had been to Ghana before. When I replied that I had worked here from 1951-53, he said: "Well, you must have noticed how the climate has changed."

Meanwhile, an interesting human story was unfolding in the south of Sudan. A rebel movement, the Sudan People's Liberation Army – which would last beyond the year 2000 – was operating in Juba where BAT Sudan had a leaf station. It was primarily a Christian independence movement opposing the Muslim government in Khartoum. Unfortunately, a BAT expatriate there called Jones had the same estate wagon model as the leader of the rebels and was ambushed and killed by government troops: a tragedy, indeed.

A little while before this incident, Jones had visited us and asked whether he could take local leave. Having divorced his wife, he said he wanted to go to Nairobi to marry his fiancée. As a result, there was a certain amount of sympathy as she stood to miss out on BAT's very generous death-in-service benefits and widow's pension. However, when Jones's wife was contacted by the Personnel Department she said she knew nothing about a divorce. She had been getting regular letters from him saying how busy he was and that he had not come on leave because of the demands of his job. It then emerged that he had recently been on leave and had set up home with a third woman, with whom he had jointly bought a house. Had he married either this woman or the woman in Nairobi and had he lived, how would he have carried on the deception? Ultimately, his widow in the UK got the pension and the other two women were left empty handed.

In Khartoum there were some unique social institutions: the Gordon Cabaret, the English Club and the Khartoum Golf Club. The cabaret, named rather blasphemously after General Gordon, was run by a Greek and featured Greek dancing and costumes. One night an inebriated colleague, Rodney Drake, got on all fours and, "bah, bah-ing" like a sheep, stopped the show.

The English Club was not large but very exclusive. Hotel accommodation in Khartoum was difficult to find and on one occasion, unable to find something suitable for a visiting senior Dutch manager, the English Club was contacted. They had a room he could have, but as a Dutchman he could not use the swimming pool.

The Golf Club was just a nine-hole course laid out in the desert with the rough being extensive and a 'graveyard' – if you hit a ball there you were in grave trouble. The tees were marked by square stones in the soft sand and to be able to tee up your ball, a strip of dry camel dung was laid on the sand. The fairways were of soft sand and the greens were brown, made up of sand mixed with old engine oil. But there was only one flag which was borne from hole to hole by the flag carrier.

Chapter Eleven

Since the 1950s the tobacco industry, particularly in the UK and the US, had come under increasing attack. Forecasters were predicting its doom as health related concerns proliferated. Conglomerates were quite fashionable and investors were urging tobacco companies to diversify. BAT, which did not have a very big presence in the UK, was slow to respond. What really aroused the board's interest, though, was the prospect of UK income and cashflow. This direct income, as opposed to dividend income, was much more tax efficient.

It was decided, therefore, that under the leadership of Desmond Misselbrook, the Deputy Chairman, diversification would take place in the UK and that opportunities were to be sought in two industrial areas: packaging and paper extending from BAT's existing businesses and fast moving consumer goods (FMCG). It was in the FMCG sector that Rawlinson and Husbands were working. Rawlinson was one of the few UK graduates employed by BAT. He had been recruited by Misselbrook and was certainly bright and fiendishly enthusiastic. But before his meteoric rise to board level and becoming the brains behind BAT's thrust into diversification, he had only worked in personnel. He had no experience of marketing, production, finance or general management. Rawlinson was a bachelor, a juvenile court magistrate, a keen golfer and, at this time, captain of Wentworth Golf Club.

Ron Peters, whose father had started an ice cream parlour in 1937, was the owner of the Tonibell ice cream business. A member of Wentworth Golf Club, he represented himself to Rawlinson as a highly-successful businessman who was challenging Unilever-Walls for dominance of the UK ice cream market. Rawlinson swallowed Peters' story, hook, line and sinker. Here was a brilliant entrepreneur penetrating successfully a significant sector of the FMCG market.

In 1964, Rawlinson persuaded the board to enter into negotiations with Peters to buy Tonibell and to retain him as Chairman and Managing Director. Peters agreed to sell for two million pounds. Extraordinarily, a director at the meeting thought that BAT had been too hard-nosed and suggested a sweetener of £250,000, which Peters gratefully accepted. Husbands was assigned to work with Peters to develop the business which, essentially, manufactured ice cream and mousse to distribute to independent, franchised Tonibell depots who sold to the public from street vans equipped with machines which made soft ice cream. This process involved expanding raw ice cream with air.

Tonibell itself only owned one factory in Boreham Wood and a few vans used in presentations to franchisers to show what a great business it was. Successful van salesmen were encouraged to become franchisees with their own depot and a fleet of vans fitted with musical chimes. Peters assisted them with their business plans, which he helped present to local bank managers, saying they had the full backing of Tonibell.

While all were Tonibell companies in name, many of the franchisees had no man management or financial control skills and many of the salesmen they recruited were pretty disreputable characters in the first place. I travelled with some of them on their rounds and it is true what they used to say about milkmen and bored housewives!

One experience which amused me involved an ice cream salesman who parked in the dark among some trees and was enjoying himself with a lady up against a freezer inside his van. A copper shone his torch in to see what was going on. On his way to the police station, the salesman asked the copper how he had spotted the van, on top of which was a cow illuminated by a small light. The copper replied he was concerned about a cow stuck up a tree!

When BAT bought Tonibell in 1964 many of the depots were struggling. No due diligence was done on them and, one by one, the depots appeared in the *London Gazette* as bankrupt concerns. I recall Langford, the legal director, coming into Husbands' office to enquire why we had bought Tonibell three months before and now it was bust. While the depot companies had been losing money, the BAT Tonibell subsidiary was making money. But the prospects were not good because new franchisees were not forthcoming.

Catastrophe struck when a visit from Her Majesty's Customs & Excise discovered that Peters had been selling ice cream and declaring it as mousse which attracted a lower rate of excise. When a senior Customs official confronted Peters with the allegation, he abused him and was ordered out of the office.

Customs & Excise were determined to see Peters in court and revealed all to BAT, which was duly alarmed. Not only would the company's first venture into diversification look inept in the extreme, but BAT – albeit unknowingly – would have been party to this fraud. BAT's export tobacco business was hugely dependent for the highly profitable Duty Drawback on tobacco re-exported and the company relied upon a totally trustworthy relationship with Customs. It was very much in BAT's interest that this matter did not reach court.

Peters was running scared and examining where he might go in the world to avoid prosecution. BAT urged him to stay while it negotiated a settlement with Customs. This they did, although Peters had to sign a statement admitting a misdemeanour. It was the end of Peters at Tonibell and the end of Tonibell with BAT. The business was discreetly closed and the assets – that is, the factory – was sold to J. Lyons in 1969. Having been paid £2.25 million in BAT shares, Peters left shortly after for Italy where he acquired the title of Marchese and changed his surname back to Pignatelli, which was the family's Neapolitan name before his father emigrated to Scotland.

Meanwhile Rawlinson was undeterred. He called an all-day 'blue skies' conference to identify another area in the FMCG sector. We spent most of the day speculating about Kvass, an ale-like drink, which was popular in Russia. It was manufactured by municipalities as well as being widely brewed in the home. Nobody around the table had tasted, or even seen it. We had no prepared statistics or information about it.

At that time, my sister Ann, a Russian scholar, was working in the research department at the Foreign Office. I undertook to see if she could provide any further information about Kvass. It only went to demonstrate the crassly-amateurish approach BAT had to diversification at that time. The day that Rawlinson organised turned out to be a complete waste of time. Rawlinson was unfortunately killed in an air crash when returning from an England-France rugby international in Paris.

Shortly after that I was appointed General Manager of BAT Holland – this involved my family moving there. On returning from the Caribbean in 1962 I had sorrowfully and remorsefully gone back to Jill, much to her mother's horror. Jill had agreed that we should try again. Although I was constantly travelling we did see a lot of each other and eventually went on a skiing holiday in early 1964 to Zermatt. Her mother still disapproved, but we got engaged there.

Jill's parents had been in Burma when my parents lived there. She and her brother – like me and my sisters – were born in Burma and we all met there in the 1930s. Jill's grandfather, on her mother's side, was a Spicer, a member of the well-known chartered accountancy firm, Spicer & Peglar. He was also the author of a book on accountancy which, for many years, was the basis of the curriculum for the accountancy exams. He had married into a wealthy Dutch family. Needless to say, Jill doesn't understand accounts!

I only discovered this connection with Holland when Jill hosted an engagement party which was dominated by these Dutch relations who had come to see how low a good English-Dutch Protestant girl could stoop to marry a Celtic Catholic. Jill's Uncle Roddy, not a Spicer and not Dutch, could see how uncomfortable I was. He called me aside and whispered that it was very reminiscent of his engagement to Jill's aunt Judy just after the War. But he consoled himself with the adage that Holland was 'a low-lying country populated by low-lying people.'

Jill's mother laid on a splendid wedding reception at Claridge's. The first night of our honeymoon was spent at the Grosvenor House Hotel before we flew off the next day to Gran Canaria where we had been loaned a splendid house in a walled garden, high up in the hills. We returned to London to live in Jill's house in Hillgate Place. Depending on whom I wished to impress, I either described my address as Notting Hill, at that time synonymous with racial riots, or the 'lower slopes' of Camden Hill. Nine months later, our daughter Joanna was born, with our son Michael appearing two years afterwards. It was a small house, and with four of us and an au pair girl, it was very crowded.

My predecessor in Holland was Drummond Forbes who was retiring. Drummond was an extremely nice man and made me very welcome; indeed, he offered to sell me his house. We liked the house and its Hilversum location because it was half way between Amsterdam and Aerdenhout, where all Jill's Dutch relations lived. The company helped us to buy it and we moved to Holland in the summer of 1967.

To be appointed, at thirty-six, as a chief executive officer of a European company was, for BAT, unusual and for me a potential poisoned chalice. Just the right medicine for a 'smarty arty' who, for four years, had been going around the group telling all-and-sundry how to run their businesses.

In the 1950s BAT had four factories in Holland with a forty-four per cent market share. In 1967 this had dropped to one factory and a market share of twelve per cent and falling. The benefits of the 1966 acquisition of Henri Wintermans cigars were still to come. Morale was very low and the 600 Dutch staff and workers believed to a man that the reason for the dismal state of business was the interference by BAT from the UK and the incompetence of the expatriates and the general management.

Drummond Forbes was not the most inspirational of managers. For starters, although he had been a prisoner of war in Indonesia with a lot of Dutchmen and the fact that he had a Dutch wife, Drummond did not speak the language. His career had been in manufacturing: all he knew about sales and marketing was the declining market share.

My first task was to gain the confidence of the management. Fortunately, Leo den Uyl, the Finance Director and Louis Price's assistant, welcomed me. By the rest I was met with scepticism and 'bolshiness'. They could all speak English, but purposely conversed in Dutch in front me. So I determined to learn Dutch as quickly as possible.

The quality of production was not a problem, neither was there any question of excessive running costs. The Dutch are frugal; they abhor waste and do not like extravagance. Our problem was that our products were old fashioned and smokers were looking for more modern products. The Rothmans group commanded the higher price categories with Peter Stuyvesant, a pseudo Virginia king size filter, and Pall Mall, a pseudo US-blend king size filter. Another of their manufacturers dominated the lower-priced category, the US-blended brand Caballero Twenty-fives.

Fortunately, after two years of striving, Drummond and the leaf manager devised blends which were a match for their rivals. But there were no obvious brand names for our new cigarettes. There existed a king size filter Virginia brand called Gladstone, which came in an old-fashioned pack and had a small but steady demand among elderly Dutch women. Surprisingly, even among other smokers, the brand carried connotations of quality. So we decided to brand our new king size filter tipped Virginia blend Gladstone Mild – 'mild' because that was a term used by smokers of Peter Stuyvesant to characterise that cigarette. It was to be packed in a US-style Twenty-five soft cup. We devised a similar strategy for our attack on Caballero. We invented a brand name, Montano, packed in twenty-fives and sold at a lower price.

Gladstone Mild Twenty-fives got off to an excellent start and Montano also began well. Shortly after the successful launch of Gladstone, at the behest of the Dutch Ministry of Finance, the manufacturers entered into negotiations to increase the price of their cigarettes. With a proportional tax rate on cigarettes, the government needed the industry's cooperation to hold prices as any cut hit state revenues. We were anxious to have an increase with an agreement that there would be no cut in prices for six months afterwards. Gladstone Mild Twenty-fives were far surpassing our expectations and it was evident that Rothmans' top managers had not yet appreciated its effect on Peter Stuyvesant Twenties.

Shortly after the agreement was signed and implemented, Rothmans woke up and applied to the courts for the agreement to be set aside. But the courts ruled in our favour. We had six months to exploit Gladstone's and Montano's growing success. But the problem was we did not have enough manufacturing capacity, despite working overtime and at weekends. The problem was solved by importing BAT crews from neighbouring countries: this enabled us to have three shifts and to borrow making and packing sets.

It was a very stimulating time. The factory managers and workers were enthusiastic and there was no argument about pay differentials for staff from various countries. I was particularly struck by the fact that our Liverpool workers, normally very difficult when it comes to changes in working practices, were no trouble at all.

Our intelligence told us that, once the agreement elapsed, Rothmans were going to market Pall Mall and Peter Stuyvesant in twenty-fives at the same price as Gladstone Mild Twenty-fives. We hastily prepared our own mild Virginia Twenty-fives, branded Belinda, which we sold at a lower price. Belinda proved a success, though not as great as Gladstone Milds. The result of this rather exciting time was that BAT Netherlands' market share – which was twelve per cent when I arrived – rose to twenty-seven per cent. Everybody had worked extremely hard and it had been worth it.

Jill and the children, meanwhile, were somewhat marooned at Hilversum, where Joanna went to a local Dutch school. Wusten, my chauffeur, collected me at 7.30am and, to avoid the evening rush hour, I would stay late at work – often not arriving home until between 7.30pm and 11pm. There were some Dutch families in Hilversum who had worked overseas and Jill became friends with them.

We did not see much of her Dutch relations, who were a disparate bunch. Teddy, who was the chairman of the country's largest flour milling business, and his wife Poolie were the patriarch and matriarch: both thin, tall and always impeccably dressed, they were sticklers for propriety. But they were also polite, welcoming and charming.

Their daughter Vonnie, who was not especially good-looking or accomplished but very good company, fell in love with Bron, Teddy's managing director. Nearing retirement, the prospect for Teddy of his MD becoming his son-in-law was a marriage made in heaven. Unfortunately, when Bron returned from honeymoon, he announced that, as marriage and business didn't mix, he would be retiring forthwith and would live on Vonnie's income. He never worked again and enjoyed a long and leisurely life. Poor Teddy worked on and on.

Apart from a dinner party or two with Teddy and Poolie, we were largely ignored by the Dutch relations. However, we were invited to a family wedding in Aerdenhout one Saturday afternoon. Confident it would be a hospitable occasion, and not wanting to drink and drive, I paid Wusten overtime to drive us there and back. We were only invited to the reception and, after queuing for some time, we eventually shook hands with the seven months pregnant 'virgin white' bride. This was followed by just one glass of sickly sweet sherry. The afternoon was very disappointing and very expensive, Wusten's overtime costing an arm and a leg!

During our time in Holland, we often left the children with the au pair and went skiing in the French Alps. We would set out in the Rover from Hilversum while it was dark and on one occasion we were whizzing along the autobahn in Germany when we noticed motorists hooting and pointing at the rear of our car. At first, I could not see the problem, but then spotted the boot cover bobbing gently up and down. We stopped at the next petrol station only to discover that the boot was half empty. Jill's suitcase, containing all her new ski and après-ski clothes, had fallen out. There was nothing for it but to return to Hilversum for yesterday's outfits!

For many years we continued to drive to the French Alps in winter. Occasionally when our map reading was faulty, we found the route blocked by snowbound passes which had been closed. I was a poor driver on icy, snowy roads - especially in Rovers and Jaguars - and my efforts at putting on snow chains were incompetent. Eventually, I bought a four-wheel Audi.

Courchevel became our favourite ski resort. For years we had the same instructor, André, who flattered my skiing. Gradually, as my fortunes improved, we moved to more expensive hotels. Our skiing was largely injury-free and when Jill did sprain her wrist she visited Dr Sex at the local clinic where he prescribed for her a 'strained wrist suppository' – *très Francais*. In my late sixties I twisted my knee badly and Jill was getting vertigo on the slopes, so we decided to give up skiing. For over thirty years when people asked "Why France?" I replied: "Because I ski like a horse and eat like Jean-Claude Killy!"

Chapter Twelve

In early 1970 I was told by Peter Tinley, BAT's director for Europe, that I would be returning to London where I would be invited to join the main board on 1st April. On that date I duly arrived on the hallowed third floor – the directors' floor – and was assigned an office and a secretary, Miss Hope-Lewis, and assumed responsibility for all BAT's interests in Africa.

Before I could even adjust my chair in the office, a board meeting was called to ratify the purchase of Wiggins Teape, a paper firm of which BAT already owned twenty per cent. Wiggins Teape wanted to expand by issuing more shares; BAT did not want its holding to be diluted and, as part of its diversification policy, decided to buy, and later expand, the company, for which it paid around ninety million pounds. A year later Wiggins Teape's head office – colloquially known as 'arse wipe house' because, erroneously, City workers thought the company manufactured lavatory paper – was sold for forty million pounds.

BAT's then Chairman, Denzil Clarke, who was shortly to retire, was a rather fierce accountant who was good at financial discipline and strong on cashflow. But he did not understand or believe in strategy which explains how BAT had become involved in ice cream and cosmetics. He was succeeded by Richard Dobson, who had a huge brain and who had been recruited from Cambridge before the war and sent to China where he wrote 'China Cycle' [published in 1946]. During the war, Dobson had a distinguished career with the RAF, rejoining BAT in 1945. He thought himself to be the very model of a modern businessman and top marketeer. In fact, he had no belief in planning or strategy and had no understanding of the role of investment in the long-term success of the business. He understood selling, but not marketing.

Dobson's intellectual superiority over his colleagues was self-evident: they were in awe of him. The one exception to this was John Ogle, the Finance Director. A muscular, stocky, bespectacled and competent finance and accounting manager, he kept a very tight control over his own managers who looked after the financial affairs throughout the group. In reality, BAT's finance department was rather like the Treasury is to the Government: in other words, it ran the company.

The other directors had different functions. Some had territorial responsibilities and in 1970 most of them could not read a balance sheet, did not understand cashflow and were unfamiliar with return on investment. If they had territorial responsibilities, the directors visited the companies checking on relations with government and communities, observing market share and distribution and seeing that factories and leaf depots were well run. But they steered well clear of getting involved with financial matters. A functional director for, say, production, monitored the state of the factories and the quality of output, but did not involve himself in productivity because it was not part of his vocabulary.

There was no attempt to compare our costs with those of our competitors. The board was only too aware that Rothmans was taking a lot of market share from our dominant position; but with the exception of John Husbands, an entrepreneur in his own right, they did not understand why.

My team consisted of a PA, who was formerly a secretary with a medium-sized subsidiary, a marketing adviser, a leaf adviser, a production adviser, a personnel adviser, an office manager and a financial adviser called Dawson, with a young assistant, Martin Broughton.

The first thing I asked to see were the budgets, profit and loss accounts, cashflows and dividend record of the companies for which I was now responsible. These companies included all the subsidiaries on the continent of Africa, but not countries where BAT was represented by importers. When I asked for this information, I was astonished to be told by my financial adviser that this was an unheard of request by a territorial director and that he would have to seek the permission of John Ogle, the Senior Finance Director, before I could see them. When I made it very clear that I was going to insist, permission was speedily forthcoming.

Broadly speaking, one's role as a territorial director was to agree the strategy, objectives and budgets for each subsidiary, review their plans for implementation and monitor their performance. The overriding requirement of the BAT board was the maximising of the cashflow to the centre. At that time, this was achieved by the finance directors in London and the subsidiary working in tandem with little regard for the long-term health of the subsidiary. Capital expenditure was very strictly controlled and dividends maximised.

In monopoly situations – and many of our subsidiaries were monopolies

- this *modus operandi* had worked well, though it did not allow a manager to develop as an entrepreneur or real businessman and, so, when competition came along, they were invariably found wanting.

The business philosophy that I tried to operate carried the simple concept that investors put money into a company today to get more money out tomorrow. This is achieved by earning a sufficient rate of return on today's investment to finance dividends and future growth. Sales growth and return on investment were vital ingredients for this philosophy.

For my first three years on the board I was a territorial director – first for Africa, then for Africa and the Far East, followed by the Far East and the Indian sub-continent (India, Pakistan and Bangladesh), then Latin America, later Australia and, finally, the US. For each of these assignments I had a different group of advisers, except for the US where heads of department (marketing, production, leaf and finance) formed the team.

The subsidiaries or associate companies reported monthly and we reviewed their performance. Throughout the tobacco group companies there was a uniform system for budgeting and accounting. I used to liken it to the ritual in the Catholic Church: anywhere in the world the Mass was the same. It was a well-tested system and did provide management at all levels with apposite information. This facilitated switching from one country or territorial grouping to another.

The more strenuous and interesting aspect of the job was visiting the countries and the companies to inspect what was going on. My first steps as a territorial director were to my old stomping grounds of Nigeria and Ghana. Nigeria Tobacco Company was a subsidiary with some ten per cent of its shares owned by Nigerians. Wootton Woolley, the Chairman, was an eccentric, self-important man. He used a monocle to enhance his image and spent an inordinate amount of time ingratiating himself with Nigerian politicians and the British High Commission. He eventually got a CBE, but he was angling for a 'K'.

While the company was not particularly well run, he was determined to Africanise it. Indeed, there were too many second-rate expatriates, particularly in distribution. He liked to show the African managers who was boss. On returning from a dinner party up-country, he asked his African PA why he had not told the host that his Chairman wanted to leave the party at ten p.m. The

PA thought that the party was going so well it would be impolite to break it up. On the journey home, Woolley told the driver to stop the car in the bush and ordered the PA to get out and walk back to his hotel.

Woolley was successful in Africanising the image of the company to the general public. He persuaded the Nigerian Broadcasting Corporation to televise the annual general meeting at the grandest hotel in Lagos. He enticed Nigerian small shareholders to the meeting, providing them each with 200 imported Benson & Hedges which in most cases exceeded the value of their dividends. The hall was packed with Nigerians who, on seeing one or two of their fellow countrymen sitting, as directors, at the table with Woolley, believed that NTC was majority-owned by Nigerians!

It was a dispiriting experience to see a company that used to make a quality product, now manufacturing poor quality cigarettes which were sent out haphazardly by un-trained and non-businesslike Nigerian distributors. The rush to Africanise resulted in massive inefficiency and an epidemic of corruption.

Woolley swam with the tide; it would have been useless to swim against it. However, I owe a debt of gratitude to him for introducing me to opera. On one of his leaves, I offered him the chance to choose how he wished to be entertained. A night at the Royal Opera House, Covent Garden was his choice and we went to see *Cavalleria Rusticana* and *Pagliacci* ('Cav and Pag'). It was for me sheer pleasure. Ever since, there is nothing I like more than a night at the opera and on one occasion I even flew by Concorde to Luxor to watch a spectacular outdoor staging of Aida with a cast of 1,500 not to mention the horses and lion, arriving back at the office in London the next morning. When I became Chairman many years later I was delighted to foster a close relationship between BAT and the Glyndbourne Opera Festival; once we came to their rescue after Sir Peter Hall had somewhat overspent on a new production!

After Nigeria I visited Ghana. The country was broke after Nkrumah and his successor had squandered the cocoa millions on extravagant 'white elephant' projects – such as the Aburi Palace – and foreign ventures, particularly in the Congo. In addition, agriculture and most of the retail sector had been turned into cooperatives and, to all intents and purposes, run by former civil servants. On arrival at Accra Airport I was invited to the VIP Lounge where, to my amazement, we were treated to pink champagne. It was clear that the economic priorities were somewhat eccentric.

One of the saddest sights was to visit Koforidua which I had known in the early fifties as a thriving cocoa district. The landscape was littered with dead cocoa trees and the villages deserted. Swollen shoot disease had ravaged the crop. Instead of cutting out these trees and compensating the farmers from the Cocoa Marketing Board's funds, the farmers had been allowed to harvest the trees until they became moribund.

When Idi Amin deposed Milton Obote in Uganda in 1971, he uttered threats about expelling Asians, many of whom had British passports. The Asians there were plantation owners, industrialists, doctors and lawyers – but most, pervasively, retail shopkeepers. Expulsion of the Asians would prove an economic disaster for Uganda but a bonus for Britain as many of those ousted became successful entrepreneurs and professional people here.

However, the British government of the day did not foresee this. Ted Heath's Cabinet wanted the problem to go away and one tactic was to enlist the help of business. Shell and BP were invited to visit Uganda, where they had substantial interests, to persuade Amin to leave well alone. The economy was going fine and it would be in nobody's interests to disrupt it.

Shell was first to go. Meanwhile, I was instructed by the BAT Chairman to embark on a similar mission. The British High Commissioner in Kampala and Trevor Tice – a great friend of Uganda and a life-long friend of mine – arranged an audience with the President. Wearing battledress, he met us in a small, unpretentious waiting room and greeted us cordially. He invited me to join him on a 'love seat' – a two-seat sofa – which was a bit of a squash.

There was a formal chat about the economy and how satisfactory BAT's business was performing. But it was not long before Amin moved on to tell us how troublesome the Acholi – Obote's tribe – were and that he intended disciplining them. Little did we realise what he meant. The other topic he wanted to talk about was the trans-African highway, which was a World Bank project. Jumping up from the sofa, Amin pointed to a map showing its route through Uganda and how he had ordered this to be changed so that it ran through his village.

Our visit was in vain. It was not long after that his reign of terror began and in August 1972, he ordered the expulsion of the Asian community. During this time, I returned to Uganda as a show of support for all our businesses which, in common with other British operations and expatriates, were being threatened.

The stories circulating about Amin's behaviour were gruesome. He had the Governor of the country's Central Bank murdered and, when asked why the Governor's signature remained on the bank notes after his disappearance, Uganda's Finance Minister explained that at least a year's supply of notes had been ordered at the time and that the bank had a six-month stock of notes in hand. "What?" shouted Amin. "Last week you cautioned me we had no money!" The minister feared for his life.

The *Two Ronnies* summed up the banality of Amin's presidency. At a time when Uganda was threatened by invasion, Ronnie Barker, portraying Amin, was asked by Ronnie Corbett, acting the role of a newspaper reporter, "What are you doing about defence?" "Good question," answered Amin. "The man with the nails comes this afternoon."

On another visit to Africa, some years later, I was at a dinner party in Nairobi organised by BAT Kenya, whose Chairman, G.M. Gecaga, was also Chancellor of the University of Nairobi. Seated near me at the dinner table was a government minister whom I overheard saying that he was also a British citizen. To say the least, I was surprised and asked him how this had come about. During the Mau Mau emergency in the 1950s he was a lawyer who had sympathised with the Mau Mau. The security forces arrested him and he was imprisoned, but had escaped and fled to Uganda. Uganda's Governor, Andrew Cohen, well-known for his Leftist leanings, was informed of his presence in Uganda and that the Kenya authorities would like him returned. The Governor asked to see him. He was informed that the country's civil service lacked lawyers and offered him a job in the government's legal department. Otherwise, he would have to be deported. Naturally, he chose to work for the Ugandans and some months later, after he had been working in the Legal Department, the Governor again asked to see him. Complaints had arisen among Uganda government officials that a Kenyan had a good post when the regulations stipulated that only Ugandans or UK citizens could hold these appointments.

There was a choice: the Governor could make him a UK citizen or he had to go back to Kenya. He accepted the offer of a UK citizenship which was expeditiously arranged. Eighteen months later he was told he would have to go on home leave and he was provided with tickets to do so, including rail tickets to and from Wigan, for in filling in his citizenship application he chose a place that would be easy to pronounce. He visited Wigan once but confided in me that he could not understand a word the natives spoke. Needless to say, the Kenyan administration at the time was not amused.

On a visit to Mauritius I met the then Prime Minister who, curiously enough, was only interested in sharing with me his concern at the high cost of funerals. I was not able to help.

After the initial success of Rothmans in South Africa, Northern and Southern Rhodesia, BAT was able to maintain its dominance in the other African countries where private enterprise manufacture operated.

Chapter Thirteen

Shortly after visiting Ghana my responsibilities were extended to South East Asia. On my first visit to Indonesia, Peter Roberts, the BAT general manager, informed me that we had been invited by the Presidential staff to call on President Suharto. At that time Suharto was living in a very modest house and after greeting us warmly he asked us to stay on for an informal lunch. This occasion was in stark contrast to the grandeur and pomp that surrounded him when he finally resigned in 1998, desperately fending off charges of billions of dollars of corruption.

On another occasion, on a visit to our factory in central Java, Jill had an embarrassing experience. Central Java is probably one of the most densely populated parts of the world. Wall-to-wall people is an apt description. Our Indonesian factory manager's wife ran a health clinic in the town and, at a reception in their house, she asked Jill if she would honour her clinic by visiting it the next day.

The visit was well organised and Jill was impressed by the various departments until they came to the birth control section. Somewhat disturbed by the evident over-population of the neighbourhood, Jill wondered how successful the initiative had been. "Well," said her hosts, "we have a problem. The Americans, very generously, provide us with free condoms, which we distribute to the *becak* [bicycle taxi] riders. But the drivers complain that they are too big and fall off. Recently, we have been supplied by the Japanese and this has solved the problem!" (One of the few pro-American stories which makes my US friends stand tall.)

Once, after a meeting with the Indonesian Minister of Finance, the BAT country finance director who was very friendly with the state security services congratulated me on the clarity of my speech. Apparently the hidden microphones had recorded every word I had said!

The country in this region that interested me most was Pakistan. The North West Frontier and its connection to the 'Great Game' is one among several reasons. Arabic language I find attractive and Islamists, on the whole, are straight forward: you know where you stand with them on deals or issues, even if you don't like what they stand for. Finally, my father preferred Muslims to Indians (Hindus). He was tempted to accept the offer to head the Finance Ministry when Pakistan was established.

Unfortunately, since the separation of Bangladesh particularly, Pakistan has never settled down as a politically and economically stable entity. It is still a largely tribal society. If anything unites the country it is the legacy of British rule, the language and the administrative system, the law and, above all, the army.

BAT owned three factories there where one would have sufficed. There was also a minority investment in a company owned by a military pension fund in the North West Frontier. Market share fluctuated between thirty-five per cent and forty per cent and there were a number of other local manufacturers. Ironically, despite the very public condemnation of smoking, our contract leaf farmers in the tribal areas were subsidised to grow tobacco as a substitute for the opium poppy.

On one visit to Pakistan I flew in via Kabul. Afghanistan was relatively peaceful at the time and driving down the Kabul River Gorge was of particular interest as it was there that the British Army, in the Nineteenth Century, was slaughtered to a man. Given the steep sided cliffs, it was not hard to imagine how. After the Pakistan frontier we drove down the Khyber Pass. The fortifications overlooking it are probably the same as 100 years ago. Many of the British and Indian Army regiments which served there had etched their insignia into the rocks by the road. The Pakistani Army still maintained them. Half way down we stopped for afternoon tea in the Officers' Mess at the HQ of the Khyber Rifles. It was very British except for the canapés. The 'Tropical Trots' the next day were more of a stampede!

In Peshawar we were the guests of the Governor of the North West Frontier, Major General Fazal-i-Haq. His residence had been built by a former British Governor and it was maintained in the same style, from furnishings and food through to servants' uniforms, portraits of former Governors and layout of the gardens. The Governor was a most engaging soldier and clearly enjoyed ruling the troublesome frontier tribes. His role was the same as before the British came to the region and since they left: that is, trying to maintain some semblance of law and order among the feuding tribes. He entertained us to an excellent dinner where wine was served. However, he did not take it: although he liked a glass, he did not trust his servants not to report him to the Imam.

The Governor accepted that his job was dangerous, not only in relation to the drugs trade, but also because of the enmity ever rife among the politicians whose comrades and relatives had suffered in the military coup which had seen General Zia become Pakistan's President in 1978. He and Zia occasionally reminded each other about these threats and consoled themselves by forecasting that they would both be tried and hanged together. Sadly, both Zia and the Governor would be assassinated.

Meanwhile, I had an ambition to travel along the old Silk Route from Peshawar to Kashgar in Eastern China. Fazal-i-Haq arranged for us to go through the Pamirs as far as the Khunjerab Pass at 15,500 feet. The road was not open to tourists and, in the event, neither was it open to us. Torrential rain had brought about a huge mud slide across the road some five miles from the top.

On a subsequent trip to Pakistan, we tried again. This time we flew by helicopter to a military camp about five miles from the summit. We transferred to a four-by-four vehicle and 400 yards or so from the top I asked to get out and walk the rest of the way. But in the thin air walking was exhausting and after 100 yards I climbed back into the four-by-four. Breathless is an apt description of the mountain scenery – whether seen by car or helicopter.

During his time as President, I had a meeting with Zia in his modest house in Islamabad. We were introduced to his family and especially his handicapped daughter for whom he clearly had a great affection. Zia was of average height, slim and quietly spoken. He was dressed in a military uniform but with only inconspicuous insignia and medal ribbons. It was a relaxed occasion and when we left I was presented with a carpet, which is now in the hall of my home in Sandwich.

India and the ITC – formerly the Imperial Indian Tobacco Company – were not my favourite ports of call. ITC was forty-six per cent owned by BAT with forty per cent in the hands of Indian quasi-governmental institutions. There was a conspiracy among the Indian management to share with BAT as little company information as possible.

The harsh and penal individual tax regime encouraged the management to enrich themselves at the expense of the company and the Indian tax authorities. BAT could not be party to this and we discovered that this misconduct was not just confined to India when one of the director's wives was arrested for shoplifting in London. Just before I retired, the authorities had rumbled the irregularities at ITC. Management and the Indian institutions used all their political capital to forestall any criminal charges being brought.

By the late 1970s commercial investment in India was penalised by their tax on dividends. The net result for BAT was that in some years our UK income from India was less than from Sierra Leone. I had a vicarious guilt complex about both the corporate and personal tax regimes. My father had been Chairman of the Board of Revenue and, in conjunction with Paul Chambers, who was sent out from the UK, the Inland Revenue introduced PAYE and other corporate systems. In ultra-socialist post-Independence India, they had used this to Draconian effect.

The other aspect of India which disturbed me was the extent of the urban squalor and poverty. I am no stranger to such things, but the vastness of number of poor in India was disturbing.

From the late 1960s to the early 1980s we took our family summer holidays at Glenbeigh in County Kerry. I first visited Kerry in the 1960s with Ben Newcombe, BAT's Chief Statistician. An Irish Plymouth Brother, Ben was rarely sober after lunch, often to be found asleep on the floor of his office with his head on a pillow of rolled up statistical charts. Above all he was a tremendous wit and frequently led me astray.

Situated on the southern shore of Dingle Bay with the Shehy Mountains towering above it, Glenbeigh was a long, deserted sandy beach and the Dooks Golf Club's course, initially nine holes, is in a spectacular position. With a ramshackle clubhouse, presided over by the amply-proportioned and congenial Molly, it was very friendly. There were two hostelries in Glenbeigh – both owned by the Evans family. The Towers in the centre of the village was run by Mrs Evans's son. There was accommodation there, but it was principally a place for drinking, singing IRA songs and dancing. Taunting British tourists was its speciality.

Mrs Evans ran the Glenbeigh Hotel, a sedate establishment where she ensured everybody behaved with decorum; the front door was locked at eleven p.m. As I was travelling most months of the year I wanted a holiday away from it all. Glenbeigh, at that time, was remote and telephone calls went through a primitive exchange which was only open for a few hours each day. UK newspapers arrived the day after they were published.

We always travelled there by car to Newport and then the ferry to Cork and car on to Glenbeigh: twenty-eight hours in all. We usually took an au pair girl with us to help with Joanna and Michael. At Glenbeigh the children played and swam on the beach, while Jill painted some landscapes and I played golf at Dooks, Killarney, Waterford and Ballybunion. There was no difficulty at that time about just turning up and playing, even at the well-known courses.

The weather makes or mars a holiday. As the children, for the first ten years of their lives, only had holidays in Ireland, the Irish weather was 'holiday weather'. Jill stoically put up with the wind and showers and, for my part, I came to believe that Irish rain was 'dry' and, indeed, to an extent it is. The rain in Kerry mostly occurs in short, sharp showers carried on a westerly wind, followed by warm, drying air from the Gulf Stream: minutes of wet followed by an hour of dry.

A lack of timeliness was another characteristic of Glenbeigh. Having a watch was of no use. Hotel breakfast from 7.30am to 9.30am was, in reality, 8.30am to 10.30am. The pub would only close when all the customers had gone. One year, on checking out of the hotel, I was startled to discover that I had overstayed by a day! Unfortunately, it was the height of the tourist season and there were no berths on the ferry.

Jill, being of Anglo-Dutch Protestant stock, was never really able to appreciate the Irish way of life. To her the women mothered too many children and did most of the work, while the men drank and chatted in the pub for most of the afternoon and night. The West of Ireland didn't seem to wake up until eleven a.m. To Jill, Irish men were drunken, layabout sex maniacs – but she married one!

There was a very Irish incident on one of our last visits to Glenbeigh. Susan was a well-constructed, blonde Yorkshire girl who accompanied us as au pair for two years. She became friendly with two brothers, former jockeys, who ran a small riding school. The year after she left us we were surprised to see her checking into the Glenbeigh Hotel with her boyfriend, a croupier. He was a slight, weedy fellow whose complexion was evidence that he seldom saw the sun or even daylight. After lunch Susan took the croupier to meet the ex-jockeys. They clearly sized up the croupier and took him trotting for three hours. It worked. Neither they nor we saw the croupier again: he was confined to his room with saddle sores!

The brothers enjoyed Susan's company until one night one of them brought her back to the hotel after eleven p.m. The front door was locked and waking the manager or Mrs Evans was out of the question. At the side of the house in the garden they spotted an open window and Susan was sure it was the lounge window and gave the brother a leg up so that he could open the window and pull Susan up.

The noise of the window opening woke up the woman sleeping in the room. Terrified by the man coming through the window, she jumped out of bed screaming "Father, Father, Father", and ran upstairs and collapsed on the landing outside the bedroom of a priest with whom she was friends. The priest and the manager attended to the fraught woman. The priest called to the manager: "Brandy! Brandy!" The manager rushed down to the bar and reappeared with a glass of brandy which the priest drank! Mrs Evans was not best pleased and threatened to report the break-in to the Garda unless Susan and her boyfriend left town before lunch – which they did.

Shortly after this incident the security situation brought our Irish holidays to an end. When we first went to Ireland it was possible to talk about 'The Troubles', but as the violence and the intimidation intensified people became more and more reluctant to do so. Nearby Cahersiveen was a hotbed of the IRA and after they had murdered a chairman of a multinational, the BAT security people advised me that they would prefer it if I did not holiday in Ireland; or, if I did, to stay in a different town each night.

By this time Jill had had enough of Irish holidays and Joanna and Michael had friends they went on holiday with to sunny Mediterranean beaches with discos. For them, the change was welcome. From then on, we had our winter skiing trips to the French Alps and I took the family on business trips to North America and Australia. While I worked, they played and I paid.

Having subjected Jill to endless holidays in the wild west of Ireland, I took a leaf from the Americans and went with her on some 'Honey-do' holidays, when instead of the husband choosing the destination, the wife does and her spouse dutifully complies with her list of 'honey we have to do this and ...'. Over the years we've been to Jordan, Libya, Tunisia, Sicily, Naples and the Veneto to visit ancient ruins and the cultural heritage. One memorable trip was to St Petersburg where we spent a long weekend enjoying the world of ballet. After watching a rehearsal and making a behind-the-scenes visit to the wardrobe and scenery department of the Marinsky Ballet, we watched a wonderful performance of Swan Lake by the company that evening. The next day there was a Gala concert with acts performed by the Bolshoi, the Mariinsky, the Royal Ballet and the Metropolitan. At one stage, Jill tugged my sleeve and pointing at a Russian male dancer exclaimed "Oh, isn't he gorgeous!" At the reception afterwards, her nerves failed her when I tried to effect an introduction and I was left chatting to the ballerinas.

Chapter Fourteen

Apart of the world that particularly interested me was Latin America. The first country I became involved with was Mexico and what appealed to me most about it were the people and their history before the Spanish conquest, the conquest itself and revolutions and political upheavals of the nineteenth and twentieth centuries. I also loved their music – the Mariachi – with three or four sad-faced Mexicans sawing away unhappily on their violins accompanied by a jolly-sounding trumpeter.

BAT had a curious two company set up in Mexico: Aguila in Mexico City and La Moderna in Monterrey. Aguila was 100% owned by BAT, while La Moderna had some Mexican shareholders. Aguila and La Moderna were competitors with no love lost between them. In the 1960s and Seventies Aguila was managed by a 'Southern Gentleman' in a typically gentlemanly style. He loved dry Martinis served in glasses taken straight from the deep freeze. The French ingredient was supplied by ringing the French Ambassador and asking him to breathe down the telephone! In contrast La Moderna had a thrusting Englishman, Ronnie Stockwell, in charge who had adopted a pseudo-American accent. La Moderna was winning the competitive battle between the two companies.

Once Philip Morris entered the fray with their powerful partner Carlos Slim and Marlboro brand, the combined market share of Aguila and La Moderna shrank rapidly. There was no longer any need to pretend that the two companies were independent and, as a result, La Moderna took over Aguila. Ronnie Stockwell became BAT's supremo in Mexico and took great pains to point out to management the sensitivity felt by the Mexican banks which held a minority stake in the business; they did not want to be bullied by management in London into agreeing strategy and investment.

At the same time, Ronnie let it be known how close he was to the State Governor and, indeed, to Mexico's President. He played this card with great conviction and was believed. Hence management in London were tentative in their dealings with La Moderna. In effect, Ronnie was running La Moderna as his own fiefdom with a minimum of oversight by BAT.

Unfortunately for Ronnie, after a couple of years the business started to nosedive. Philip Morris was eating into La Moderna's market share and Ronnie resisted, on nationalistic grounds, all offers by BAT for expert assistance. It became obvious to myself and Brian Garraway, the then Finance Director, that Ronnie had to go. But with his high-powered political connections, how could we ease him out?

Brian and I decided to go on a secret visit to Mexico to talk to the bankers, politicians and lawyers about how we could get rid of Ronnie without damaging La Moderna. To our amazement, it transpired that Ronnie had no special political connections. The bankers had been disappointed that BAT had shown so little interest in its troubled subsidiary. We flew on to New York and summoned Ronnie to meet us at the BAT apartment in Essex House, overlooking Central Park.

Ronnie went quietly and the problem then was to find a replacement. La Moderna's in-house Mexican lawyer seemed the best candidate and, being a lawyer, seemingly the most trustworthy. Unfortunately, a few years later he contrived in conjunction with a friend of his to gain control of the company. Some years on BAT had to buy back the company from this gang for eighty million dollars: a sorry tale!

It was around this time that an amusing incident took place at the Essex House apartment. BAT's lawyer, a small, very dapper man, who was staying there, was breakfasting wearing only a towel around his waist. Finishing breakfast, it was convenient to leave the tray in the corridor outside the door- this way one wasn't disturbed by the maid when she came to collect it. However, as he bent down to place the tray on the floor, the front door – which had a very heavy spring – began to close, catching his towel. Within a second, and to his astonishment, he found himself outside the apartment and absolutely naked. The apartment was at the end of a very long corridor. He failed to gain the attention of other guests leaving their rooms so he unloaded the tray and, using it to cover his front, he knocked on the door of the next suite. A woman opened the door, shrieked and went back inside; but she did telephone for help.

An interesting Central American country I visited several times was Nicaragua. The first visit was when the country was run by Anastasio Somoza in the period before the earthquake in 1972 which totally destroyed the capital

Managua. I was surprised by the urban and rural poverty which reminded me of Ghana. My next visit was after the national liberation group, the Sandinistas, had ousted Somoza in 1979 but were being besieged by the rebel Contras.

BAT had a 100% market share in Nicaragua, a country whose economy had been hard hit by the political turmoil. In a small industrial area of Managua most of the factories were closed. The rich Managuans, who had owned some of them, had fled. The multinational companies – almost all American – had been expropriated, but the Sandinistas did not know how to run them. BAT was the only multinational operating without disturbance: even the distribution system was allowed to continue. The reason for this apparent immunity was that cigarette excise was a major source of revenue. The Sandinistas preferred to rely on BAT's honesty in collecting this excise than entrusting its collection to the 'sticky hands' of their cadres.

We were advised that there was no danger in walking or driving in Managua or in the countryside. It was ironic, therefore, that when a minister came to lunch with us in the office that he was accompanied by a posse of very heavily-armed soldiers. The irony was reinforced when we visited the US Ambassador. The Embassy was heavily guarded – not to stop anyone getting out – but to stop asylum-seeking Nicaraguans getting in.

The third time I visited Nicaragua was after the Sandinistas lost the 1990 Presidential election, when Managua had been destroyed by an earthquake and the city was derelict with scrubby bushes growing in the ruins. This visit was memorable for a meeting with the President – Violeta Chamorro, a handsome, gentle and quietly-spoken woman – who was sitting in a rocking chair as she received us in her modest office. In more senses than one, she seemed too good for the uncouth, macho Nicaraguans. She didn't last long. Sadly, the high ideals she fostered for the country's development failed to come about and the Sandinistas returned to power, this time democratically elected. Nicaragua was another case of the failure of the bourgeois democracy model favoured by the Americans that left the vast majority of people in Central and Latin America stuck in the poverty trap.

Chile became my favourite South American country. However, on my first visit, it was sad and rundown place with a rapidly failing economy. Allende had been elected President and his Socialist policies had led to a flight of capital and a total halt to foreign investment. Many of the bourgeois entrepreneurs had fled, large haciendas had been appropriated and agricultural production had plummeted. It was not a happy country and tension was prevalent.

While BAT enjoyed 100% of the Chilean market, the management felt beleaguered. BAT's income from Chile had dropped from five million dollars per annum to $50,000 per annum. My visit was designed to show continued support and was very much welcomed by the management. As in Nicaragua, the Socialist government had not interfered with the running of the company as it provided a reliable source of excise.

Some six or seven years later, when General Pinochet had overthrown Allende as President, I returned to Chile. By this time the Chilean company was prospering under its Chairman, Hernan Cubillos, who had been Navy Minister in Pinochet's first Cabinet. He had arranged for me to have an audience with Pinochet. While there, we were the President's guests and had to accept his protection. It started at the airport where we were met by a protocol official and ushered straight into a limousine which, accompanied by a motorcycle escort front and rear, took us to our hotel.

The whole top floor had been commandeered and our suite was surrounded by rooms occupied by plainclothes security personnel. When Jill went shopping, she was accompanied by an escort of motorcycle police, much to her embarrassment. I had the same treatment when I attended Sunday Mass, to the consternation of the congregation.

A meeting with Pinochet had been arranged, but before this we visited our factory at Valparaiso. This trip was even more embarrassing as oncoming cars, buses and lorries were all directed to the side of the road and into ditches to allow us through. It was not a journey to win the hearts and minds of our customers. If only they knew. Fortunately, on the return journey the Presidential helicopter was put at our disposal. The seating onboard was as sumptuous as in a first class cabin of a Jumbo Jet.

On the penultimate day we went to La Modena, the Presidential Palace in downtown Old Santiago for the meeting. Our delegation consisted of myself, a Chilean colleague from London and an interpreter. Cubillos did not join us. We were ushered into a waiting room which looked out on to the Plaza. These rooms had been restored after being destroyed by Chilean fighter-bomber planes in the attack during which Allende had died – either from his injuries, suicide or the hand of a murderer.

An aide took us to meet Pinochet who greeted us at the door of a large, elegant room. He was accompanied by his *aide de camp* and two ministers. At the far end of the room was a semi-circle of upright chairs, with the Presidential chair in the middle. We were asked to sit. Pinochet had a rather florid complexion with a good crop of silver hair and was dressed in a light brown suit. I waited for the President to make the customary trite remarks welcoming us to his country. But not a word. Then my interpreter nudged me and whispered: "Say something to him. Say something." So, I did. Pinochet nodded, again said nothing and indicated to one of his ministers to reply. The meeting ended without Pinochet uttering a word. It was a bizarre experience.

On a subsequent visit to Chile, Cubillos had arranged that we travel to Peru via Bolivia. As Jill was again with me, Cubillos's wife and daughter joined our party which included BAT executive Ronnie Creighton and his wife. We met up in the Peruvian capital, Lima, before flying to Cusco to visit Machu Picchu the following day. The hotel in Cusco was a renovated monastery and the city itself is about 8,000 feet above sea level and Jill promptly collapsed with an altitude headache while the rest of us retired to the bar where, beside our chairs, was an oxygen cylinder from which we took whiffs between sips of Dom Perignon.

Then we had bad news. The workers of the railway company, which was the only transport to Machu Picchu, were on strike. Cubillos said he would see what he could do; and, sure enough, he arranged for the management to drive the train, but we had to leave before dawn as the pickets would not be out then. How he did this I do not know: I never asked. We boarded the train before light and, just in case of trouble, so did a squad of soldiers. But there were no patrolling pickets as we chugged out of Cusco.

Approaching Machu Picchu, but still some way from it, we ran into a three feet mudslide; some of us tried digging it away, but it was a hopeless task. The general manager who was driving the train said that the only way to remove the mudslide was with a bulldozer. But the bulldozer driver was on strike too. Somehow, he was persuaded to arrive with his machinery and remove the mudslide and we travelled on to our destination. There were no other tourists in Machu Picchu on a sparkling day and we had the great pleasure of exploring the site on our own. On the return journey we left the train five miles from Cusco and bussed to our hotel where the other tourists were more than somewhat frustrated at not being able to visit Machu Picchu.

We flew on to La Paz in Bolivia where we boarded the train to cross the Alto Plano down to Chile. But it was no ordinary train. The passenger carriages at the front were the usual basic over-utilised and over-crowded, shabby rolling stock one associated with Third World countries. Attached to these were three contrasting carriages. The first was a Pullman with sleeping cabins, kitchen and dining room; the second and third were recently-renovated general manager's cars each with bedroom, bathroom, sitting room and balcony. Jill and I were assigned one of these.

The Alto Plano is just that, a high featureless plateau. Along the way we passed a tin mine where the Patino family made all their millions. Although it took about thirty-six hours to reach the border with Chile, the food and wine were excellent and with congenial friends it was a memorable trip. I was surprised how little interest was taken in us by those crowded in the front carriages of the train. They would have had every right to be envious and taciturn.

However, some unpleasantness did show itself at the border. All the passengers at the front had to get off the train with their baggage and wait at the side of the tracks while their luggage was inspected by the Chilean police. Meanwhile, we were left in our carriages which were coupled with another engine and were off into Chile to a chorus of very loud and well-deserved boos from the other passengers. Our next stop was Chile's largest copper mine where we were accommodated in the manager's palatial house. The military were in charge of labour relations and there was no trouble with the workforce.

Around 1986, I visited Paraguay. We did not have a factory there, but Paraguay, like Singapore, lived on the *entrepot* (a trading post where merchandise can be imported and exported without paying import duties) trade. Compared with its neighbours – Argentina, Peru, Uruguay and Brazil – duty on goods in Paraguay was very low and smuggling into these adjoining countries was the main source of income. Cigarettes and whisky had been the mainstay of this trade; but now it was cameras, electrical goods and women's luxury accessories. Nevertheless, there was still a substantial trade in contraband cigarettes. Of course, BAT knew that its products were being smuggled. We sold to importers who sold on to others, some of whom were smugglers.

Recently, sanctimonious western governments have condemned multinational companies for being involved in this trade and in Britain the

Labour government even looked into the possibility of prosecuting BAT. They did not succeed and it was absurd that they should have even tried. If the smugglers could not get their merchandise in Paraguay, they would get it somewhere else, which is even truer today with globalisation. What right has a western government got to try to dictate to another government what its export policies should be, as long as it is not being harmed by it?

As far as BAT was concerned, smuggling was often to our disadvantage. For example, in Brazil our market share was eighty per cent; smuggling, therefore, affected BAT's position, particularly as the popular smuggling brands were from other major manufacturers. Smuggling may not be the oldest trade, but it must be the second oldest. But, along with prostitution, it will be around for ever.

At the time of our visit, Paraguay's capital, Asunción, was a small town reminiscent of the 1930s. No high-rise buildings, quiet and sleepy, it was a very macho town: men ran everything and women knew their place. They kept out of sight, even in the home, though maybe not in the bedroom.

General Alfredo Stroessner, the country's dictator since 1954, had been in power for over three decades. A meeting had been arranged with him and around 8.30am we assembled in a remarkably inconspicuous single-storey building, to be ushered into a small, crowded waiting room. The others there were the members of Stroessner's Cabinet whom he was seeing first. It was a meeting with the Cabinet, rather than a Cabinet meeting. They chatted very affably among themselves until they were called in one by one to the General's office. When summoned, most straightened their ties and rubbed their shoes on the back of their trouser legs.

Finally, it was our turn. Accompanying me, apart from our agent, was our Chilean director, Ronnie Creighton. Stroessner rose from behind his large, wooden desk to greet us. He was of medium height and build, wearing a light grey suit, a good head of dyed black hair with a neat moustache. Ronnie was anxious to ingratiate us with the General and told him that we had just come from Chile where we had a positive meeting with his friend, General Pinochet.

Ronnie went on to explain that, because of my Irish descent, I had long wanted to come to Paraguay, where my Irish heroine, the beautiful courtesan Eliza Lynch, had been the lover and mother of the six children of the country's nineteenth century president, Francisco Lopez, thus becoming a national icon in the bargain. This struck a chord with Stroessner who revered Eliza and had been responsible for arranging for her remains to be brought to Paraguay from Paris in 1986. After recalling some of her exploits, he invited me to visit her grave and place a wreath there. An aide was despatched to arrange it.

As we left the General's office we were informed that the visit to the Cementerio de la Recoleta would take place at noon. Arriving there we were met by a detachment of troops, a group of photographers and the most enormous wreath. I had expected a mausoleum-type tomb, but the grave itself was modest; the wreath overwhelmed it. However, I was glad to pay tribute to this remarkable woman.

Brazil was a country that had always fascinated me. I have mentioned that, as a management trainee, I opted to be stationed there. Souza Cruz was BAT's most successful company. Its market share was eighty per cent plus, achieved with a range of good quality brands distributed by a model sales force. Its six factories were efficient and productive, based on excellent relations with the workforce. Souza Cruz had developed with small farmers a tobacco leaf business which provided leaf both for the local market and, importantly, a crop for export.

During and after the War, Souza Cruz was managed from the US, with the senior management being Americans. In the 1970s this changed and there were a succession of UK expatriate chief executives – Teddy Rigby, Eric Bruell, Tom Long, Ken Sumner and Peter Rombaut. These 'expats' were followed by Brazilians.

I enjoyed my trips to Brazil. One of BAT's more successful diversification ventures took place in Brazil which was the substantial investment in the Aracruz eucalyptus pulp plantation and mill. Over the years I witnessed Brazilia developing from a raw, muddy building site into becoming a major city. I called on three or four of the country's leaders there: one, President Collor, who was later disgraced, was a particular friend of Peter Rombaut.

You have to attend the Carnival of Rio to really appreciate what a fantastic spectacle it is. But it is not for those who like to go to bed early. Each day for three days, it starts at six p.m. and often doesn't finish until eight o'clock the following morning.

The contrast between the poverty in the north east and the relative affluence of the central and southern states is a huge problem. I went with Peter Rombaut to Bahia for his marriage which the Cardinal there had agreed to celebrate privately. The Cardinal discussed with us the area's main social problem of 400,000 street children: and Bahia was just one of the vast northern eastern towns.

The mining company Vale invited us to visit their iron ore mine in the Amazon Basin. It was a geological phenomenon: a huge mountain sticking up from the jungle producing very high grade iron ore. The ore was a dark rust-coloured shale which had the same texture as a rusty shipwreck.

At the confluence of the Rio Negro and the Amazon rivers we watched the aerobatics of pink dolphins and in the Mato Grosso we spent a fascinating weekend at the Pantanal national park, which is one of the world's largest wetlands. The rivers there were home to huge otters – eight to ten feet long – alligators and other rare species.

Not so rare in the creeks are the piranhas. Our Brazilian host caught some and placed freshly-cut sticks between their teeth. They had no problem in biting through the sticks with one snap of their jaws. Just on the opposite side of the sandbank to where we caught the piranhas, our host was swimming. I was invited to join him and did so reluctantly. The secret was to swim in the fast-flowing water. We took a lot of piranhas back to the estancia where the cook used them as ingredients for a soup. It was a memorable weekend.

When doubts arose in the international investment community about the trustworthiness of Brazil, I was determined to support the country and when I became Chairman of BAT I spoke reassuringly at conferences and seminars about how Brazil had always honoured its obligations. For this, the Brazilian government honoured me.

Imasco [Imperial and Associates Co] was the diversified associate company of BAT in Canada. Like all BAT companies it was originally a tobacco company – Imperial Tobacco. During my time on the BAT board, it was headed by Paul Paré. Imperial Tobacco was the leading cigarette company with a market share in the 1970s of thirty per cent to forty per cent, which steadily grew until the 1980s when it reached sixty per cent. In the 1970s it followed BAT's diversification by buying a drugs chain, Shoppers Drug, which became very successful – and a sports goods business.

Under the nationalist policies of Pierre Trudeau's Liberal government, foreign-dominated companies were not able to buy more than forty-nine per cent of substantial Canadian businesses. As a result, Imasco was discouraged from diversifying in Canada and looked, instead, to the US, where it had no management and a limited source of finance. BAT already had its own company, BATUS, which was diversifying in America and the possibility of conflicts of interest arising was unattractive.

The real absurdity of the Canadian government policy was that it was an economic contradiction. The government was doing a lot to encourage foreign investment and Imasco wanted to re-invest in Canada and BAT wanted it to do so but not without a controlling stake of fifty-one per cent. So by default the only option for Imasco and BAT was to invest in Canada's neighbour and rival, the US. So Paul Paré arranged for us to meet Trudeau at his office in Ottawa to discuss our dilemma. He was sympathetic and charming, but non-committal. He suggested we talk to his Commerce Minister, Herb Gray.

Gray had graduated from being a trade union leader to national politician. He did not like big companies and particularly multinationals. We met him one evening at his local party office in a scruffy building in a suburb of Toronto. He wanted to encourage foreign investment, but it had to be on Canadian terms. He would not accept that these were uncompetitive and we got nowhere.

So, Imasco bought an American fast food chain, Hardee's. Unsurprisingly it was not a success. Subsequently, Canada - under Prime Minister David Munroney - relaxed this absurd policy and Imasco bought Canada Trust bank in 1986. This was a very successful investment culminating in its sale to Toronto Dominion for eight billion dollars in 1999.

It was always a pleasure to visit Imasco for the board and management were confident, professional and very open. Discussions were invariably frank and friendly. Indeed, many of the top executives - especially Paul Paré - became friends. Paul and his wife Audrey regularly invited us to their homes - particularly their farm in Ontario. In turn, they joined us one year on our skiing holiday in Courchevel. Paul was an obsessive tennis player and at his farm he would assemble guests to play hour after hour with him. He had a love-hate relationship with golf and on more than one occasion I have seen him literally break a golf club in anger on the course. Being somewhat temperamental myself, I could sympathise.

Imasco sponsored both the annual Canadian Tennis Open and the Canadian Open Golf Tournament. The US and Canadian professional golf associations do not permit professional golfers to receive fees for appearing in their tournaments. But where there's a will, there's a money-paying way. To attract top US golfers to the Canadian Open, Imasco held the Chairman's Tournament the day before the official Pro-Am. Some of the leading golfers were paid as much as fifty thousand to sixty thousand dollar. Three of Imasco's business friends were in a four-ball with one of the professionals.

Each year I was invited to take part and had the privilege of playing with Jack Nicklaus (twice), Lee Trevino, Tom Watson, Greg Norman, Fred Couples, Scott Hoch, Ben Crenshaw, Raymond Floyd and Curtis Strange. Most of these had won the Masters at Augusta and, as I had played in Europe with Nick Faldo and Seve Ballesteros, also winners of the Masters, I used to boast that "in order to play with Sheehy in the Chairman's Tournament you have to have won the Masters!"

Almost all the pros were enjoyable company, interested both in you and your game. Trevino was the one exception. He tended to play to the gallery rather than with us. At dinner after one tournament, when I had played with Watson, I queried with Trevino whether gripping tightly with the left hand only, as I had been taught, was just for club golfers and that professionals gripped firmly with both hands to achieve greater control and distance. Trevino replied: "It's dinner and, while I don't like to be dirty, the only thing I use my right hand for is to wipe my arse!" That's Trevino. Scott Hoch, who described Faldo as having a 'charisma bypass', had self-evidently had one himself. Even so, in my experience, his description of Faldo was accurate. Faldo spoke with us on the first and eighteenth holes and for the other sixteen he might as well have been playing by himself.

Paul and Audrey Paré had four adopted children, whom they cherished. When their eldest got married and went to live in Zambia, they planned to visit her. Having worked and travelled a lot in Africa, I advised them to buy a 'Tsetse Belt' to ward off sleeping sickness. Imagine my consternation when, some months later, passing through London on his way to Zambia, Paul phoned me and asked in all earnestness where he could buy a 'Tsetse Belt'!

This reminds me of a time when I first went to Africa; I used to claim that the kit we were recommended to get included a 'gonoscope'. This resembled a stethoscope, but with the middle rubber tube somewhat longer so that you could put it on the end of your penis and listen for the 'clap'!

Pro Am: Jack Niclaus on my R

With Mark McCormack on my R and Arnold Palmer on my L

Pro Am: Seve Ballesteros on my L

Pro Am: Greg Norman on my R

Tip O'Neill on my R; Congressman Dan Rostenkowski on my L

Tom Watson on my R

The perfect cartoonist's model

Members of the Inquiry into Police Responsibilities & Rewards
L to R: Prof Colin Campbell. Prof Eric Caines.
self, John Bullock. Sir Paul Fox

The butt of jokes

NEC TIMIDE NEC TIMORE

The Armorial Bearings of
SIR PATRICK SHEEHY
of Eldon Road in the Royal Borough of
Kensington and Chelsea, Knight

College of Arms,
MCMXCI

Hubert Chesshyre
Chester Herald.

My investiture at Buckingham Palace – a team effort

Chapter Fifteen

When Peter Macadam became Chairman in 1975, I was appointed his Deputy, with BATUS and Canada [Imasco] as my territorial responsibilities. Apart from Brown & Williamson [B&W] and Export Leaf, BATUS owned Kohls retail stores [1971], Saks Fifth Avenue [1973] and Gimbels [1973] and as well as Appleton Papers [1978], all acquired as part of the diversification strategy.

Richard Dobson had not been confident in BATUS' ability to own and run department stores, even though they provided the finance and, to that extent, were accountable, so he called in a retail specialist Lawrence Hill to determine how they should be run. Macadam dispensed with him and the US retail business reported to BATUS management, which was headed by Joe Edens, another delightful southern gentleman whose background was the manufacturing side of the tobacco industry. Neither he nor I knew anything about the retail business, but we had to learn fast as BATUS retail interests were in a parlous state.

Saks had suffered from years of under-investment and was losing market share throughout America to Neiman Marcus. The four Gimbels divisions were a shambles with two of them out of control. BATUS owned eighty per cent of Kohls, with the rest owned by the founder Herb Kohl who used this to block any constructive attempt by BAT to actively engage with the business. Herbie was Chairman and Chief Executive of Kohls, but though the company was well run, it was more for his own short-term interests and not for those of BATUS. He did his utmost to keep BATUS out of the strategy or management of the business. Both Saks and Kohls had growth potential: Saks in the high fashion market and Kohls in the supermarket business. Saks' Chief Executive Alan Johnson was a long-time manager there and was desperate for it to be revitalised.

In the US, corporations which have major and minor shareholders often find that the two categories have different objectives and strategies. Minor shareholders frequently resort to litigation with the courts tending to favour them. Herb Kohl was aware of this. A bachelor, something of a 'loner' and very much a Milwaukeean, on the face of it, he was apolitical. So it was something of a surprise when he became a candidate for the US Senate and was subsequently elected.

Eventually in 1986, under my watch as Chairman, BATUS sold its shares to a consortium which successfully and dramatically expanded the Kohls chain. The 'minority' lesson was duly learned with Kohls and, thereafter, we always required 100% of companies in the US.

The situation with Gimbels was altogether different. It consisted of four independent divisions: New York, Philadelphia, Pittsburgh and Milwaukee. Each had flagship, downtown department stores with satellite stores in the suburbs or in other towns in the state. Almost the only thing each store had in common was the Gimbel name: even the logo was different in each division. Each had its own management system and buying organisation and advertising. There were no synergies.

The competition was fierce, coherent and with centralised direction, projecting a unified and consistent statement, offering better value for money and a far greater range and service. They were also making better profits. Gimbel Milwaukee was in profit with a broadly positive cashflow; Pittsburgh hovered between breaking even and a loss; New York and Philadelphia were both loss-making and haemorrhaging cash.

Retail 'shrinkage' - a trade euphemism for theft - was alarming. It was hypothesised that half was customer theft and half stolen by staff. Shrinkage in both New York and Philadelphia was extremely high and often involved 'big ticket' items such as carpets and furniture, with staff probably colluding with suppliers. The bulk of the workforce in these divisions was unionized and it was an open secret that the unions were being manipulated by racketeers.

'Markdowns', too, were also a major problem. The management information systems were so inefficient that stock control was chaotic. Buyers could not purchase using any reliable information - there was suspicion of collusion between buyers and suppliers. Gimbels would receive supplies even for their over-stocked positions which would then be marked down at the store.

While other chains were expanding into the new, affluent suburbs, Gimbels was stagnating and losing market share in its existing areas, with one exception. A mall was opened in downtown Philadelphia and Gimbels anchoring one end of it. The new mall was opened by the city's notorious Mayor Frank Rizzo and afterwards there was a celebration dinner at the hall where the US Declaration of Independence was signed. Rizzo made a typically robust speech linking the event that day with the Founding Fathers, although I cannot recall how he contrived to do this.

After a number of management changes aimed at sorting out the mess in these divisions, we closed them down. The net result of the closure was some $300 million for the real estate. We should have done it years earlier and concentrated on Saks. A statistic which constantly amazed me was that twenty per cent of the Saks' customers accounted for eighty per cent of its turnover. Many wealthy women spent as much as $100,000 a year and, on occasions, special customers were given the privilege of shopping after closing time. Often they would arrive with suitcases full of dollar bills which were emptied to pay for their purchases.

We did spend a great deal of time and money renovating existing Saks stores and developing new sites in new cities. Saks CEO, Alan Johnson, was able to surround himself with a team of first-class managers because of the introduction of a competitive earnings structure. Top talent recognised the potential and were excited by the prospect of sharing in the future success of the company. One of the most dynamic and outstanding managers recruited by Saks was Bob Suslow who formed a great partnership with Alan Johnson and the store went from strength to strength.

Marshall Field and Co, the famous Chicago chain, came on the market and, as we believed it could be run better and had growth potential, we decided to make a bid. At this time, Bruce Wasserstein, who died in 2009, was just making his mark in Wall Street mergers and acquisitions and his firm was heading our bid. There were other players – particularly arbitrageurs and, most notably, Ivan Boesky.

Brian Garraway and I would fly to New York, arriving at our offices at seven p.m. and negotiate sometimes into the early hours with Boesky and his team. Wasserstein eventually procured Marshall Field for us for $400 million. We installed new management and the fortunes of the store group began to turn around. In Illinois, Marshall Field retained its well-respected up-market franchise.

Previously, in November 1977, I had been invited by British Airways to join the inaugural Concorde flight to New York. Primarily backed by US airlines and manufacturers, New York State had tried to prevent a Concorde service to New York, so when we landed there were no national, state or city representatives at Kennedy to meet us and, as there had been little publicity, neither was there a crowd to cheer the arrival of this remarkable aircraft. However, British Airways had arranged a group photograph of the VIP passengers. Somehow, much to my embarrassment, I accidentally knocked Lord [Hugh] Scanlon off the stand and he had to go to hospital. This was followed by lunch in the huge ballroom of the Waldorf Astoria, crowded with businessmen and bankers. There is no such thing as a free lunch and I had to make a speech to this illustrious gathering. Poor Hugh was not on the return flight.

Over the years Brian and I frequently flew Concorde. After leaving Heathrow on the 9.30am flight, returning on the same day on the 1.30pm New York service. We would arrange a meeting at British Airways' Conference Centre at Kennedy Airport, much cheaper than getting merchant bankers and lawyers to travel first class to London.

Acquired in 1978, Appleton Papers had been identified by BAT's subsidiary company Wiggins Teape, the UK and European leader in carbonless paper, as having the lion's share of the US market. From the marketing and technical side, Wiggins and Appleton worked closely together. BATUS monitored Appleton's plans - agreeing budgets, financing and business benefiting from the cashflow. It was a single-product business, well run, growing and with a good return on investment.

Appleton had a plant within a couple of miles of the Three Mile Island nuclear power plant near Harrisburg, Pennsylvania, where, in 1979, through a fault, there was an accidental release of radiation. This resulted in a lot of scary stories and local property prices plummeted upon talk of closing the plant and having to decontaminate the surrounding area. In the event the radiation was confined to the reactor building. Within six months property prices recovered and the plant was reactivated and is still operating today. Laymen had feared that the accident was the result of the plant failing; in fact, it was the failure of staff to operate the plant properly.

If concerns about Appleton's plant were soon allayed, there were big problems with B&W, BAT's US-managed tobacco business. In their highly-profitable market, they were gently losing share, year by year. B&W had three significant brands: Viceroy, its leading full-flavour filter brand in the early 1950s; Kool, which had led the menthol market; and Raleigh, the leading coupon brand in what was a small and static segment. Marlboro was already attracting the bulk of new full-flavour, filter smokers, while Salem and Newport were rivalling Kool.

The basic problem was not smoking quality – that is, taste – but product quality. The manufacturing standard of BAT brands was far inferior to that of Philip Morris or Reynolds. When the filter trend exploded in the US and started developing worldwide, these companies together with Rothmans had identified that Molins' making machines produced a far better quality product than the rival Hauni. They had cornered the market in Molins' machinery, while B&W had equipped itself with Hauni.

The main drawback with Hauni was that the tobacco was not tightly packed. Either the packaging machine rejected the cigarettes, which had to be ripped and the tobacco returned to be used again, or the smoker got a cigarette which was loosely filled, smoked harshly with tobacco left in the packet. It was a vicious circle.

The more 'smalls' – as the recycled, ripped tobacco was called – the more cigarettes were rejected. When I took over, the "smalls' accounted for fifteen per cent of a blend, when the maximum should have been three per cent. The reject sensors in the packing machine had been adjusted to rates for cigarettes with loose ends, so that the smoker got a consistently-poor product.

The damage had been done, although a new Production Manager from BAT research and development had diagnosed the problem. This coupled with productivity far below that of our competitors, factories in Louisville and Petersburg that were in old, multi-storey buildings unsuitable for installing new tobacco and cigarette-handling equipment and machinery were all part of the problem.

The Production Manager had persuaded my predecessor, Peter Macadam, that the optimum solution was a new factory on a new site in the major tobacco-growing area of Georgia. As a result, a new $150 million factory at Macon was being fitted out with the latest machinery, which would solve the quality problem. Jimmy Carter was the Governor of Georgia when the factory was being planned and he was mightily pleased and proud at the significant investment in his state and near to his home town.

Even after he left the Presidency, on a visit to London he invited me to lunch in the City and later sent a gracious letter. He and his wife did not approve of smoking, but he liked the tobacco farmers and large employers in his state.

Like other cigarette producers, B&W was very active in lobbying Congressmen and Senators in Washington in order to ward off legislation that could harm the industry. Stu Spencer's firm was our principal lobbyist and very effective he was too. He had many interesting and amusing stories about vote rigging in the early years after World War II when the election process was easily manipulated.

Closely involved with helping Ronald Reagan win the Californian governorship, Stu went on to serve as Reagan's presidential campaign manager in 1980 and served as a trusted adviser to the President in both his terms. He famously told the *Los Angeles Times* that 'politics is never a science, it's always an art.'

Each year I used to spend three or four days in Washington visiting Senators and Congressmen who were either pro-consumer and the tobacco industry, or were neutral. We also used to play golf with some of the Republican politicians at the Burning Tree Country Club. The regime of this club is surprising given how close it is to Washington DC, the world capital of Women's Lib! For not only was it an all-male membership served by an all-male staff, but women were not allowed on the property, with one rumoured exception. On the Saturday before Christmas women were allowed into the Pro Shop to buy presents for their husbands.

Among the politicians with whom I played golf, the most eminent was Senator John Warner; it was apparent how he charmed Elizabeth Taylor. We regularly called on Jesse Helms, the North Carolina Senator who championed tobacco growers. Contrary to his public 'tub thumper' image, he was a quietly-spoken, gentle person, though his views were far from gentle. He despised Communists and Socialists and during one visit to his office he urged me to prolong our chat so that he could keep the Socialist Belgian Defence Minister waiting.

Another Washington moment came at a Johnny Cash concert at the Kennedy Centre, where our party was seated prominently in the VIP Box. I fell asleep which was cynically remarked upon the next day by a Congressman from Tennessee.

Stu Spencer's influence was such that he was able to arrange for an invitation for Jill and myself to attend a State Banquet at the White House on the occasion of President Mitterrand's US visit. Before dinner we all lined up to be introduced to President and Mrs Reagan and President and Madame Mitterrand.

There were a number of round tables in the Dining Room and on our table I was seated next to Barbara Bush, whose husband George was then Vice President. To her right was the French Foreign Minister, M. Cheysson, a Socialist and, apparently, anti-American. Half way through the meal, Mrs Bush turned to me and said, "Pat, please talk to me. If this little Frenchman keeps insulting America, I will hit him!" She had recently visited Ethiopia, so we chatted a lot about that and also discussed her missionary zeal for spreading literacy in the Third World.

During the dessert course, an ensemble of violinists from the military played tunes from musicals of the forties and fifties. Two or three of the violinists were women, which prompted Cheysson to remark: "Madam Bush, I did not know that you had so many women in the Marine Corps!"

After dinner we firstly retired to a large room with a small stage where Julio Iglesias, Mrs Reagan's favourite performer, entertained us. After this, a band assembled in the hall and the President and the First Lady led the dancing which was constantly interrupted by ladies saying 'Excuse me'. During the evening a Senator from Louisiana asked me why, as a Briton, I was attending a banquet for a French President? I had no answer.

President Reagan was, indeed, a great communicator. The first time he impressed me was when he ran against Jimmy Carter for the presidency and in a short television spot he addressed the camera in a head-and-shoulders shot and said simply: "You know folks, people say that Jimmy Carter is doing his best. And that's our problem!"

I was especially impressed by Reagan's favourite joke about the Soviet Union, which he told at a Claridge's luncheon in London during talks with Margaret Thatcher:

A Russian went into his local Lada car dealers and told the salesman he wanted to order one. You do realise it won't be delivered for ten years and you have to pay for it now, he was told. "Yes," said the customer, "and here's the money."

"But just one question," he added, "what day will that be?" "We guarantee today's date in ten years' time," said the salesman. "Will that be morning or afternoon?" "Why are you worried about morning or afternoon in ten years' time?" enquired the salesman. "Because I've got the plumber coming in the morning!" came the reply.

Speaker Tip O'Neill was another with whom I played golf. He was rather reluctant to talk politics and when he did have something to say it was littered with foul expletives. He was an unattractive character.

Joe Eden, Chief Executive Officer, and Charlie McCarthy, Chief Operating Officer, were both golfers and, one way or another, we managed to play most of the major American courses – most unsuccessfully.

One winter Stu Spencer arranged for us to go skiing at Lake Tahoe. I did not think much of the skiing or the gambling joints. One of the slopes had just been sold to the Japanese by one of the 'Toni Twins' – the identical sisters who found fame after appearing in TV ads for Toni hair treatment products with the slogan: 'Which twin has the Toni?'

One of the twins had a large house where we stayed; a fellow guest, a Federal judge, was wooing her. The other twin came to the house the following morning to help with the breakfast. When the judge swept downstairs and into the kitchen he spotted the twin with her back to him at the sink wearing tight trousers and proceeded to 'goose' her. Much to his embarrassment it was the wrong twin!

Apart from the 1977 acquisition from Lorillard of the overseas licences for their brands including Kent which was to become one of BAT's great success stories, major developments initiated by B&W during my time included the introduction in 1981 of the Barclay brand and with B&W assuming responsibility for US exports and US brands for overseas manufacture.

Barclay had an innovative 'Actron' filter which reduced the tar and nicotine without diluting the taste. It launched so well it alarmed Philip Morris who were driven to claim that the filter did not reduce tar and nicotine, but merely cheated the machine that measured their contents. B&W denied this but the subject became one of public controversy and affected Barclay's credibility and sales.

For years Philip Morris and Reynolds had been actively developing an international demand for their US brands, Marlboro and Winston. BAT's international business was managed from a small department in London which was almost exclusively interested in selling State Express Filter Tip and Benson

& Hedges Filter Tip. It sold B&W brands in export markets when they were ordered; it did not market them.

The international demand for US brands was growing much faster than UK brands, but there was no restructuring of the company to address this missed opportunity. It was quite apparent that our German company, that had assumed responsibility for the export of its own brands, had had considerable success. When I was in the Netherlands I insisted that BAT Holland should develop its own brands in export markets and we did sell a reasonable quantity of Gladstone Mild in some markets.

So, responsibility for US brands was handed to B&W and shortly after the chance was seized to buy the rights to the Kent brand outside the US, which strengthened the international portfolio.

I spent a lot of time with B&W management, travelling to these export markets. One really profitable market where the company had particular success was Japan. For many years the Japanese market had been closed to imports. Even when this was lifted there were restrictions on distribution and promotion. For example, you were only allowed to advertise brands in the language of the country of origin. But through constant pressure from the US government these restrictions were blown away and a sizeable market for imported cigarettes emerged.

On one of my trips to Japan I decided we should spend a weekend skiing in Sapporo. The resort was similar to Lake Tahoe with a series of smallish, independent ski fields. I was impressed by how fashionably-dressed the skiers were and even more impressed by the exploits of Yuichiro Miura, the man looking after us who had skied down the highest mountains in every continent. We saw a video of his expedition to Mount Everest which contained dramatic shots of him skiing down from 24,000 feet.

In contrast to the British and to the West generally, one could only admire the immense achievement of Japanese manufacturing after the War. It was to the credit of Japan's industrialists that they were willing to share their experiences. As Chairman, I arranged for the management of our major companies to spend two weeks in Japan, visiting various industries to study their product innovation and development, manufacturing systems, distribution and marketing. It was a rewarding experience.

However, I found the formality of negotiating with Japanese management irksome. I also disliked the obsequious bowing, inane pleasantries and obscure proposals that took place before you eventually got to the substance of any meeting.

Japan is such an overcrowded country that even the pin tables are vertical and not horizontal – as in the West – presumably to save space in the Pachinko parlours. And it is not very different in the hostess bars located on every floor of the high-rise city buildings. Overcrowding is such a problem, too, that young couples live for years with their parents or in-laws because of the scarcity of housing. To get privacy for procreation they book into 'love hotels'. And on the subject of intimacy, our party attended a Geisha ceremony where I found a yawn was certainly not as sexually arousing as I mistakenly thought.

Chapter Sixteen

By the early 1980s I moved on and up from being the Chairman of the tobacco companies to become Deputy Chairman and a member of the Chairman's Policy Committee which, effectively, was the policy-making and oversight body for the group associates and subsidiaries' activities. The other members were Peter Macadam, Chairman, and John Simmons, Finance Director. I still retained a particular responsibility for worldwide tobacco operations.

In 1982, I became Chairman of BAT Industries which had become the parent company's name in 1976, reflecting the fact that only half the Group's business was then in tobacco, with the balance being in paper, cosmetics and retailing. Ever since becoming involved in BAT's diversification, I had not been convinced that any one of the sectors we had been in would give the company current and future growth to match that of the twentieth century. Brian Garraway, our Finance Director, was very much of the same view.

The carbonless paper business of Wiggins Teape and Appleton had a finite life as plain paper copying technology was proving to be its death knoll. Department stores were losing out to specialist retailers and the cosmetics division, run by Eric Morgan who had been put in by Dobson, took up an enormous amount of management time far in excess of its value to BAT. Peter Macadam had rather liked the glamour of the cosmetics industry but, with little room for growth or expansion, I sold it.

In stark contrast to all the above, retail financial services, whether insurance or banking, offered huge expansion and growth opportunities worldwide. It was also by definition in the consumer sector. The board agreed that we should seek opportunities in this sector.

While we were looking, Allianz, a large German insurer, made a hostile bid for Eagle Star in 1984. It seemed a good candidate for financial services diversification and it would enable us to get a foothold in UK retail financial services. Eagle Star was seeking a 'White Knight' and enthusiastically accepted us as potential owners. Many of their investors and policyholders were Jewish and were not keen on the idea of German control. The battle for the company was quite drawn out, but polite. Allianz eventually conceded that we could and would pay more and we did. Our final offer of £968 million marked the largest takeover in British corporate history to date.

The late Sir Brian Mountain was the entrepreneur who had developed Eagle Star into a substantial insurance company. He had two sons, Denis and Nicky. Denis did not get on with his father and did not work for many years in Eagle Star. Nicky, on the other hand, started at an early age in the company. When Brian died, Denis – no doubt because of his big shareholding – joined the company as Executive Chairman. His main interest was in the very large property investment portfolio; his expertise was in hunting, shooting and fishing. The company's marketing was non-existent.

I was surprised at the first board meeting that only the minimum of formal business was conducted before the board – which consisted mainly of representatives of major or former customers – retired to lunch. The Eagle Star cellar and table was renowned in the City. I enjoyed some shooting and stalking on the company's estates in Hampshire and Scotland. In truth, Denis treated them as if he owned them.

Meanwhile, Brian Garraway was trying to get to grips with the business. The structures within Eagle Star were very informal. The business plan and budget were vague. There had been no management recruitment or training policy. We brought in Michael Butt, who had an insurance broking background, to succeed A.R.N. Ratcliff, Eagle Star's General Manager, as Managing Director.

All this was too much for Denis who was allowed to retire early on the grounds of ill health. I don't think he ever understood the business of selling insurance or the risks that went with it. Talking of the Mountains, I had asked Cecil Parkinson, the Minister for Trade and Industry, to lunch at BAT but meanwhile the Sarah Keay's affair broke. I thought it churlish not to maintain the invitation even though he was no longer a minister and he accepted. He asked how Brian Mountain was and I replied that he had been dead for some years and that his son Denis was running Eagle Star. Expressing how remiss he was at his mistake, he told us how a Labour MP kept referring to him in the House as Michael Parkinson. Finally he confronted him in the lobby and said: "If you want to get it right, remember Michael's the one with the vasectomy!"

The Eagle Star property portfolio was gradually re-shaped. Unfortunately, the company became a victim of the property boom of the 1980s by offering a unique new product, the mortgage indemnity, which sold like hot cakes; but in the 1990s when property prices slumped, the product proved a disaster and Eagle Star was left nursing a £1.2 billion hit.

Eagle Star survived but Michael Butt, who had enthusiastically launched the mortgage indemnity product, left and returned to broking where he was very successful.

A year after acquiring Eagle Star, BAT was approached by Mark Weinberg to see if we would buy Hambro Life [later renamed Allied Dunbar], the retail insurance business he founded with Syd Lipworth and Joel Joffe. He had a business with, justifiably, a first-class reputation and expansion potential. They were very protective of their staff, particularly the sales reps, and he wanted to continue to have a major say in the running of the business. This was in contrast to the management of Eagle Star.

Mark joined the BAT Industries board more out of curiosity than any interest in developing the BAT financial services strategy. When Sir James Goldsmith's Hoylake Investments consortium came along with a hostile bid for BAT, he resigned explaining that his friendship with Jacob Rothschild gave rise to a conflict of interest. As soon as the Hoylake hostile £13 billion bid had been seen off, he started up St James's Place, a clone of Allied Dunbar. This new company backed by Jacob Rothschild, a member of the Hoylake consortium, intended to lure the top-performing sales team away from Allied Dunbar. In hindsight, we should have locked Mark in with a two year term and a non-compete clause.

In 1988, through BATUS, we pursued our financial services strategy by making a hostile bid for Farmers Insurance, the eighth largest US insurance group. Farmers had a curious structure: it did not own the Exchanges which carried the risk; but it did manage these exchanges which were, in effect, mutuals. The corporation had been steaming along sedately and profitably under the investors' radar. But Cravaths, Swaine and Moore, the New York law firm specialising in M&A, had spotted Farmers' potential with it being undervalued.

Farmers' management was not receptive to our approach and believed that their good relations with the many state insurance commissioners would enable them to argue that to be owned by a tobacco company was too risky, especially with the potential liability from smoking and health litigation. To counter this, we had to recruit law firms and lobbyists in each of the fifteen states where Farmers operated. In turn, Farmers had their army of advisers and along the way some very unpleasant things were said about BAT to the commissioners.

Ultimately, our team did a brilliant job in portraying most of Farmers' arguments as irrelevant to the issue. One of the trickiest moments came when Farmers explored our behaviour in the Third World and came up with what looked like a blemish in South Africa. Shortly before our bid, there had been a vociferous international media campaign condemning multinationals for employing Africans below the subsistence level line. BAT had been cited as one of the culprits. Farmers seized on this and went to the Catholic Bishop of Birmingham, an outspoken anti-apartheid opponent, and got him to condemn us to the press, radio and television. In fact, there were only two individuals – both youths and unmarried – who were paid marginally below the subsistence line. Even then, this line did not apply to them as it was meant to be for a married worker with two children.

When this was pointed out to them, Farmers did not pursue the matter further. But it irked me that a Catholic bishop should intervene in an M&A battle. Accordingly, we hired a detective agency to check how many employees of Catholic private schools in South Africa were paid above the subsistence level. It surprised us that not many of the teachers – let alone the gardeners and other domestic staff – were paid above this level. An appropriate letter was sent to the Bishop of Birmingham, copied to Cardinal Hume, and the Catholic Church said no more about the subject.

The denouement came at Farmers' annual meeting in California. Our request to address the delegates was turned down. Our lawyer replied that we would be arriving with a bull horn. They admitted defeat and welcomed us. It became a mutually-rewarding partnership.

BATUS became a model of BAT diversification strategy in investing in successful retail, paper and financial services companies. IMASCO in Canada had diversified with retailing, pharmacies and sporting goods, but was not very successful in fast food with Hardee's in the US. But in 1986 it bought a thriving financial services retail business, Canada Trust.

The Souza Cruz holding company in Brazil, Compania Souza Cruz

Industrio e Commercio, had also performed strongly with a very successful pulp and paper business among others.

Our Australian associate Amatil had no real strategy other than to invest in any business which Australians were good at! Its investment in Coca-Cola franchises, both at home and abroad, was outstandingly successful. However, its investment in cattle ranching for beef exports was a disaster. At one time Amatil seemed to own half of New South Wales and three-quarters of Tasmania. Many of the farm properties were very attractive and I and my colleagues took time out to visit them. It was amusing to hear us 'City Slickers' discussing cattle breeding and other ranch topics of which we were blissfully ignorant.

BAT Germany invested in retail [Horten] and plastics. Horten was the third largest group of department stores in Germany with the most growth opportunities. The problem was that that the sector was static, trending to decline and in those conditions expansion and profitability were very hard to come by.

Another associate which had diversified was the Indian Imperial Tobacco company. But BAT had virtually lost control of this subsidiary. The management had their way by manipulating differences with shareholders. I had long believed that the only investors to make money in India are Indians – and I have yet to be proved wrong.

But we needed UK income and had to invest here. My predecessors had embarked on retail investment by buying International Stores, an ailing grocery business which was converting its medium-sized shops into self-service supermarkets. Its management was ageing and clearly lost in the rush by the likes of Tesco, Sainsbury and Asda. Although International Stores was almost as big as Tesco, their rival stores had much better offerings.

We made numerous management changes and tinkered with re-shaping the property portfolio, but never had the ambitious vision of Tesco. Consequently, International Stores just limped along despite the additional acquisition of Pricerite's 130 stores. It was derided by the investment analysts who held it as an example of BAT's inability to manage a retail operation.

However, one entrepreneur interested in our retail side for the property opportunities offered by the restructuring was Gerald Ronson. He was a good man to do business with: he wanted any deal to be condensed to one side of a sheet of paper and there was never any haggling afterwards. His word was his bond. Ours had been a business relationship, so it came as a surprise when Jill and I were invited for a long weekend on his 4,000 ton motor yacht 'Gail IV'. Others invited included David Scholey of Warburg's, but he had to cancel at the last minute for the 'Guinness Affair' was beginning to simmer.

We flew to Nice in Gerald Ronson's private jet where we boarded the yacht. Ivan Boesky and his wife arrived in an extra-stretched limousine which housed not only their luggage but also a portable trampoline. Our host announced at dinner that we were not to 'talk shop' but then proceeded to do so endlessly. Boesky, who always carried a little purse attached to his wrist, soon relaxed over dinner and told us this story against himself.

Boesky said he had come from nothing and despite achieving world fame in finance and becoming an international benefactor of the arts, he had never achieved any sporting skills, even though he had tried golf, tennis and skiing. Then one night at a party he met an Austrian count whose sport was carriage driving. Intrigued and thinking that if the Duke of Edinburgh could do this he could, too, he sought to find out more. The sport seemed not to require much physical effort and, having talked to the count, he decided this could be the sport for him. He had a large estate in up-state New York where he could keep the horses and carriage and practise driving. The count was appointed as consultant and he ordered six horses for the estate. On their arrival, the count asked about the stables. "Stables?" Boesky replied. "I thought I might keep them in one of my fields." The horses were sent to livery and the carriage was housed in the garage; all was deemed ready. So, the count began his coaching with one horse bridled. But after thirty minutes of stumbling about the field with the horse out of control, Boesky decided this was yet another sport not for him!

Boesky did not stay for the whole weekend but disembarked at St Tropez. A month later he was charged with Wall Street insider trading fraud. I have often wondered whether during that weekend on the yacht he was cooperating with the Securities Exchange Commission and if that oblong purse contained a tape recorder.

As we lay anchored off St Tropez, a thirty-foot motor launch came alongside just before lunch. Up the gangway appeared Gerald's great friend and business collaborator, Philip Harris, (later to become Lord Harris of Peckham) the carpet millionaire, together with his wife and their daughter and her partner. The lunch and conversation was convivial and as the Harris party were leaving they were invited to return for dinner. Knowing that Gerald liked people to dress for dinner, Mrs Harris said they could not because they only had their beachwear. Gerald would not accept this. Pointing to the shore, he said St Tropez was infested with fashion boutiques. That evening the ladies appeared smartly and fashionably dressed for dinner, while admitting that they still had their swimsuits on as they could not find any knickers to buy in St Tropez.

Gerald then got caught up in the Guinness insider dealing affair and when he came out of prison, he asked me to his usual annual lunch. In his speech he recounted how he had lost weight at Ford and caught up with a lot of reading. As I was leaving, a journalist said to me: "Did you notice the preposition? You either say you were at Eton or in prison!"

In 1962, BAT had made a fifty per cent purchase of printers Mardon Son & Hall which specialised in packaging for the tobacco and other industries. Desmond Misselbrook, who was Deputy Chairman and the architect of diversification, actually liked to be referred to in public as Chairman of Mardon. By the time I became Chairman, Misselbrook had long gone and many of these early acquisitions were being reviewed.

Mardon was seen as not really fitting and only having limited potential; so it was decided to put it up for auction. Robert 'Captain Bob' Maxwell had made a great success turning around a huge West Country printers and was in the market for Mardon. He put in a significant offer by letter, but his attention switched to completing a deal to buy the Mirror Publishing Group, owners of the Daily Mirror. His first and much-trumpeted priority became the Daily Mirror and the profile it gave him: he built a helicopter pad on the roof of its Holborn headquarters and employed Peter Jay, Britain's former Ambassador to the US, as his personal assistant.

I eventually received a call from Maxwell asking to see me about the Mardon auction. He was sure we could do a deal and avoid mergers and acquisitions fees. As his bid – contained in a letter – was considerably higher than any other, I suggested that, as the seller, it would be protocol for me to visit him.

So, the following afternoon, I met Maxwell and he proposed a price some thirty per cent lower than the bid figure in his letter. He expressed astonishment at the contents of the letter and claimed that it had not been authorised by him.

He told Peter Jay to arrange some tea for me while he investigated the matter with his colleagues. After twenty minutes he returned to confirm the letter was unauthorised. It was Maxwell's way of doing business. Mardon Packaging International was later sold to its management for £267 million, at the time the UK's largest ever management buyout.

Some years later I was invited to an Anglo-Israeli dinner at which Maxwell was to be the speaker. On arrival we were told he was ill and that one of his sons would read the speech. In fact, Maxwell had jumped off his yacht into the Atlantic to avoid prosecution for wide scale fraud.

A happier UK diversification was Argos. Peter Longland, one of three Finance Directors of BAT Industries, brought the opportunity to us. Richard Tompkins, who founded the company, had had a heart attack and been advised by his doctors to retire from stressful business activities. It was a relatively small operation of catalogue showrooms with one even smaller competitor. Longland believed and persuaded us that it had considerable potential and that, as the asking price in 1979 was only £35 million, it was not a great risk. He was right. It was a highly-engineered business capable of rapid organic expansion, combining market research with logistics all within computer systems that housed showroom sites, catalogue selection, purchasing, stock material and re-ordering, labour scheduling and accounting. It was profitable from day one, and when, after Hoylake, we demerged it, its value was some £605 million.

Chapter Seventeen

As the process of expanding into the financial services sector together with reassessing our retail and paper portfolio gathered pace, in July 1989 I became nervous because for two to three weeks there had been unusual activity in our shares. Unfortunately, our stockbrokers, BZW, did not have a ready explanation but we were obviously aware of the assault in America on R.J. Reynolds (RJR) by the private equity firm Kohlberg, Kravis and Roberts (KKR). In those heady days, I had even been approached by a merchant banker proposing that I should lead a management buyout.

Nevertheless, I was surprised to receive a call from Jimmy Goldsmith saying his Hoylake consortium, whose other key members were Jacob Rothschild and Kerry Packer, was announcing a bid for the company and could he come to see me. Goldsmith had attempted to buy the company in the 1970s. Imperial Tobacco, which owned twenty-six per cen of BAT, was diversifying out of tobacco at the time and was proposing to sell its shares to him. This had alarmed BAT and a committee of the board, which included me as a younger member, met a committee of Imperial, including its Chairman and Deputy Chairman. It was a very frosty meeting. If the word "treachery" was not used, it was strongly implied. Imperial did not pursue the transaction, though in subsequent years they did divest themselves of BAT shares in two or three tranches. They lived to regret it.

On receiving Goldsmith's challenge, I immediately called Brian Garraway. We agreed we had to see him off, so we called in our merchant bankers, Lazards and Warburgs, and our brokers, BZW and Cazenoves. Our first tactic was to get the support of as many substantial banks as we could, so denying Hoylake the financial backing they needed. We also decided to enlist Goldman Sachs and Shearson Lehman to act for us in America. Apart from our US retail and paper interests, Farmers' Insurance was vitally important to our future there.

A few days after Hoylake's initial announcement, I received a call from Ronald Artus at the Prudential telling me that at least ten of our major shareholders wished, as a group, to talk to me. They came to my office and spelled out in no uncertain terms that they wanted Hoylake seen off. They were particularly scathing about Goldsmith. Did they have suggestions about how to go about it? No. With expensive merchant bankers at our disposal, it was up to us to come up with the solution.

It soon became clear that the biggest obstacle Hoylake faced was satisfying the Insurance Commissioners in the many US states where Farmers operated that Hoylake was sufficiently well financed to own Farmers. From the outset, Hoylake realised this too, and one of its first moves was to get a waiver from the UK Takeover Panel freeing it of the expensive necessity of underwriting its bid until the Insurance Commissioners had given the go-ahead from the American end.

The Panel's Chairman, Lord Alexander, was a great friend of Jacob Rothschild and in our view should have stood aside. As it was, the hearing became a 'stitch-up'. Alexander had written the decision before the hearing. It meant that we had to go to considerable expense to defend ourselves, including motivating our staff for a bid that might never happen.

A very frustrating feature of these early days was that Goldsmith was able to ridicule BAT Industries, while our advisers told us not reply. Our management could not understand this. The Hoylake bid was notionally worth £13.2 billion, which made it the largest the UK market had seen. We launched the first round of our defence in mid-August. Our circular to shareholders, '*A British Success – A World Class Performance*', pointed out that B.A.T. Industries shares had handsomely outperformed other blue chip companies in recent years.

Just before I stood up to speak at the Analysts Conference, we played a line from a Beatles song that went 'you never give me your money...you only give me your funny paper'. It was a light touch with a serious point, as the bid was very hard to value. Our presentation demonstrating how well our businesses had performed under our active management ensured that the Hoylake offer only received a derisory level of acceptances from our shareholders.

The Insurance Commissioners were the key and we retained New York lawyers Cravaths, Swaine and Moore to mastermind our determination to persuade the Commissioners that Hoylake was not suitable. Hoylake, realising it had an uphill struggle on its hands, did a deal with AXA, whereby the French insurance company would be joined in their bid as future owners of BAT Industries' insurance interests.

At this time, both in the UK and America, public relations consultants were employed to cast doubt on the suitability of Hoylake. This was not difficult in the US because Goldsmith had been renowned for his 'greenmail' activities – where enough shares were purchased in a business to threaten a takeover – which, politically, proved very unpopular.

In each state we retained a local law firm and a local consultant, while in Washington Stu Spencer and Bill Hecht did an outstanding job of lobbying senators and congressmen. Orchestrating this dispersed team was a major problem: everybody had to sing to a similar tune. We had regular meetings in New York, sometimes with each state personally represented, but more often with telephone calls. It was reminiscent of the Eurovision Song Contest ("Come in California!" "Come in Oregon!").

Meanwhile, back in the UK, in late September we published our own proposals to reshape B.A.T. Industries, entitled *Building Shareholder Value*, a five step plan aimed at releasing value to shareholders and accelerating our plans to focus on tobacco and financial services, which was seen as the growth business of the twenty-first century. It was clear that investors had become unhappy with conglomerates and, as we had already agreed to divest ourselves of retailing and paper in stages, we now decided to do it all at once.

Both Argos and Wiggins Teape Appleton were to be demerged, with the shares being given to our shareholders, while other non-core businesses were to be sold. Tobacco and financial services accounted for some 80 per cent of the Group's profit but the demerged businesses had real scale, as both went straight into the FTSE 100 Share Index in their own right.

The proposals to reshape the Group, which also included a higher dividend pay-out ratio and a ten per cent share buyback, were put to shareholders at an Extraordinary General Meeting in October and they received overwhelming support. Despite this, Hoylake continued attempting to win the support of the US Insurance Commissioners, succeeding in some states but mostly not. California was crucial, being Farmers' home state. When Hoylake failed there it was really the end.

It was not an easy decision to sell these companies. Their managements valued their inclusion in BAT Industries and many had supported us publicly in our battle. The one consolation was the very good prices we received. This surprised the analysts who could never understand how a conglomerate operated. We were mostly followed by tobacco analysts, despite our substantial interests in retailing, paper and financial services. I suspect that analysts in these latter fields would not earn bonuses from passing information to their tobacco sector colleagues who, in turn, would not want to share their bonuses with them. The result has been that conglomerates can thrive in the Far East but are an extinct species in the West.

My successor, Martin Broughton, eventually demerged the financial services, merging them with Zurich, and BAT reverted to a classic tobacco business. So, as I said at a 'Hoylake 20th Anniversary Dinner', there were three players in the Hoylake contest: BAT Industries, Hoylake and the advisers. Both BAT and Hoylake were losers. Hoylake had lost and paid the price. BAT fought so that we could preserve our future in financial services, but the battle cost us ninety million pounds and financial services were eventually demerged. The advisers were the winners, enjoying high fees over fifteen months. Was it ever thus?

My strategy of a combination of tobacco and financial services served BAT shareholders well and to this day I have kept my BAT and Zurich shares. Both have performed splendidly.

Chapter Eighteen

In 1989, the Berlin Wall came down and the Soviet Union collapsed, events which unlocked huge markets previously inaccessible to BAT. I was tremendously excited by these new developments and set off to search for new business opportunities before the competition got there first. My first visit to Eastern Europe was to the former East Germany. A year earlier America's CIA had estimated that within some five years the East German economy would rival that of West Germany. It was patently obvious that this was rubbish. Ever since then I have had no faith in CIA economic pronouncements.

Everything in what was former East Germany seemed run down and shabby: the roads, the towns, the industries and the shoddily-built apartment blocks. The contrast with West Germany was stark. A profitable market for cigarettes in a unified Germany would depend on a substantial economic revival which, it turned out, would take a long time.

Russia was a huge market that opened up. Under the old Soviet Union, most of the cigarettes sold there were manufactured in Bulgaria. Little tobacco was grown in the Soviet Union, while the Bulgarians grew a large amount of air-cured and oriental tobacco. My initial visits to Russia were with a delegation from the European Round Table of Industrialists. On our first visit we met a small group of ministers and bureaucrats to discuss the framework for foreign investment. The second came at the time of President Gorbachev's attempted 'Great Leap Forward' in foreign investment and he wanted us industrialists to outline our plans.

I was invited to present these for tobacco and indicated that the quality of Russian American-style cigarettes ['americanski'] as opposed to the traditional long-tubed papyrosi was abysmal and that better-quality cigarettes could be sold at higher prices, so enhancing government revenue. Russia should have its own manufacturing industry, rather than relying on imports from Bulgaria, which had become a state independent of the old Soviet bloc, and that with modern, high-speed machinery, the Russian market would need only four factories, rather than fifty or sixty inefficient small factories. At the meeting, Gorbachev dismissed it all as impractical for what would they do with all the people who would have to be laid off. Shortly after he was called away and the discussions degenerated into an unstructured melée.

Meanwhile, our German colleagues had been beavering away identifying possible factories and brands that might be available to foreign investors in Russia. The possibility of acquiring one or two became real when Gorbachev decided to privatise large swathes of Russian industry and resources. The method was to give shares to the workers in these plants, mines or oilfields. There were no proper valuations and no proper market for these shares. Inflation was rampant. The workers needed cash and did not understand the potential value of their shares and were ready sellers. But wily entrepreneurs and top management did; the latter also made sure that, in some instances, we did not get a look in.

So we were sent off on a wild goose chase to Siberia in search of a new site for a factory. We flew to a gaunt city where we stayed in a solid but charmless hotel. The next day we boarded a large helicopter in which the pilot and co-pilot smoked non-stop from take-off to landing. The door was open throughout the flight to our destination, a small town just across the Europe-Asia dividing line.

It was a unique spot. Eighty to ninety per cent of the population was of German extraction and most were more fluent in German than in Russian. From the late nineteenth century Germans had been urged to settle in the Crimea and southern Russia as they made good farmers. But, above all, they became more skilled industrial workers than the Russians and Stalin's industries needed them. During World War II when Hitler's troops threatened the Crimea, the Russians forcibly evacuated these German settlers to Siberia. There they set up industries which had now become redundant, hence the opportunity for a new cigarette factory. But it would come to nothing.

Upon unification, the German authorities offered to welcome all Russian-Germans back to the homeland. I have often wondered how many took up the invitation.

After we had discussed the possibility of a factory with the local community, we were invited to a picnic in a nature reserve. So we again boarded the helicopter and landed in a field of buttercups surrounded by a small forest. Set out was a big table with white tablecloth and chairs organised by two large maidens with kerchiefs on their heads, altogether an idyllic Russian scene.

There were, of course, endless toasts with inane speeches and faces at the party grew more and more red, not from the sun but from the vodka. The main course was bear meat with the bear having been shot the day before in the nature reserve! Our helicopter pilots enjoyed both the meat and the drink but we flew back without incident. After lunch I went for a walk and came across some barbed wire fencing and a watchtower. On enquiring, I was told it was a former gulag. BAT did eventually buy the Moscow factory from the management and another in Saratov.

Around this time we were approached to take part in a British Week in Moscow to coincide with the Queen's visit. It was suggested we sponsor *As You Like It* directed by a modern British dramatist at the small Bolshoi Theatre. I was not too keen on the production in question and as it was showing at a provincial theatre in England, some BAT staff went to see it – an all-male affair with modern dress and a stark set - we were persuaded to sponsor it, but I made it clear I would not be attending. This was considered to be unfortunate as we would get less benefit if I did not host a reception.

Our PR agent had spotted that, as part of British Week, some top British chefs had been despatched to Moscow to demonstrate British culinary excellence. They came up with the proposal that we should sponsor a Great British Banquet, which was a splendid idea. We hired the dining room of the best hotel in Moscow for what was to be a 'black tie' affair. We also hired a small group of British actors to entertain the guests after dinner. But to make it really British – apart from port and cigars – we believed we should have haggis; but haggis without a piper would be a shame. Where to get a piper?

Just opposite our offices in Westminster there happened to be a piper playing in the street outside the Army & Navy Stores. Much to his surprise he was asked if he would like to come to Moscow to pipe in the haggis at the Great British Banquet. He agreed. But unfortunately on the night, while working in the kitchen he had too many vodkas and his entry with the haggis was somewhat delayed and far from steady! Nevertheless, the banquet was a great success. It was over-subscribed and those attending included two ministers. One guest had no black-tie outfit and, instead, hung a 'no smoking' sign about his neck!

It was around this time that I received an invitation from Prince Michael of Kent to meet him in Kensington Palace to discuss our Russian plans. On arrival the butler ushered me into the drawing room and went upstairs to get the Prince who from the sounds of it was clearly asleep. He came down and told me how useful he could be in helping the company in Russia as he spoke the language fluently and was well-known there. Before a fee was mentioned, I assured him that we were in good hands already and thanked him for his kind offer.

Hungary and Ukraine were two of the countries where we acquired companies early on. Visiting the factory in Ukraine, I discovered it was three to four hours from Kiev, the capital. There was plenty of farmland there but little agricultural activity. The villages were not dissimilar to those in the Third World – in a word, wretched. The ministers we met seemed out of their depth: Moscow was no longer telling them what to do. In Poland, where in 1995 we purchased another factory, the ministers and government officials were altogether more confident and easy to get on with. Our Jan III Sobieski brand proved a winner.

I also went to Moldova and Macedonia. The Moldovans were frustrating to deal with, but we were shown a vast underground complex of tunnels where huge quantities of wine were stored. In Macedonia we were led a merry dance. While, in a room on the ground floor of their factory, they were discussing with us local manufacturing of BAT's international brands, on the second and third floors they were producing counterfeits of our brands for smuggling!

We were invited to discuss the privatisation of the tobacco industry in Bulgaria. I had visited Sofia some years before and had stood in line to view the body of the country's first Communist leader, Georgi Dimitrov, only to be reprimanded on a cold day by a colonel and told to take my hand out of my pockets. This time the atmosphere in Sofia was more relaxed. The senior management of Bulgartabak, the state-owned monopoly to whom I gave my presentation of how BAT was organised and operated, listened, asked me questions and took no action.

⁂

In 1985 I was invited to a banquet at Windsor Castle for the state visit of Dr Hastings Banda, the President of Malawi. It was a grand occasion and I felt very privileged to attend. The Princess of Wales was there, looking radiant and strikingly beautiful. Nine years later I attended another dinner, this time at Buckingham Palace, for the state visit of Robert Mugabe in May 1994 during which he was awarded an honorary knighthood. I had been knighted myself in 1991 and so I arrived proudly wearing my 'K', my Chevalier Legion d'Honneur and my Brazilian National Order of the Southern Cross – a rather large star - only to be trumped by my old friend Algy Cluff who inquired whether he could buy a similar decorations down the Portobello Road! During dinner my stiff white shirt burst open. Fortunately the ever-resourceful staff at the Palace managed to patch me up and after dinner I was summoned to speak to Mugabe in the presence of the Queen and the Duke of Edinburgh. Mugabe was nowhere to be seen and I overheard their Royal Highnesses wishing that he would go to bed.

That same year I received an invitation to join the Queen and Prince Philip for a private lunch at Buckingham Palace. The Court Circular pages of twenty-fourth of March 1994 recorded it. 'The Queen and the Duke of Edinburgh held a Lunch Party yesterday at Buckingham Palace. The guests were: Miss Helena Bonham Carter (Actress); Miss Patricia Scotland QC (Barrister); The Hon Peter Benson (Partner, Coopers and Lybrand); Dr Gordon Beveridge (President and Vice-Chancellor, Queen's University, Belfast); Mr John Hanson (Director-General, British Council); Mr Ian McGeechan (Former Rugby Coach to Scotland and the Lions); Mr Bruce Pattullo (Governor and Group Chief Executive, Bank of Scotland); Sir Patrick Sheehy (Chairman, BAT Industries Plc).'

After assembling and being briefed by a courtier on 'the correct form', we knew when the Queen was joining us because the corgis arrived first. It was all very homely with the Queen feeding them biscuits under the table. She told me how concerned she was about her next major public engagement, her visit to the Normandy beaches and battlefields on the fiftieth anniversary of D-Day and the fact that her children were reluctant to become engaged with the event. All in all it was a very pleasant and agreeable occasion, certainly for Prince Philip who sat next door to the entrancing Miss Helena Bonham Carter.

Chapter Nineteen

I was delighted when in 1993 BAT Germany set up a meeting with Uzbekistan's President Islam Karimov in Tashkent, as it meant we could visit the ancient cities of the Silk Road whose history fascinated me. The existing factory was in Tashkent, but the President sought to persuade us to build a factory in Samarkand, his home town. The Tashkent plant had been built by the Soviets in the 1950s and was one of the factories showed off to visiting statesmen, including Fidel Castro. It might have been built in the 1890s the machinery was so decrepit!

The President duly arranged for us to visit Samarkand, Bukhara and Khiva which all lived up to my 'Arabian Nights' expectations, especially the latter which was the best preserved. In Bukhara we saw the Emir's Palace, a little way outside the city. I was intrigued by the harem and the large pool alongside it with its gazebo-like structure where the Emir sat watching his wives bathing. It was said that he would have oranges thrown into the pool and the first wife to retrieve one was his companion for the night. I developed this into a game for my grand-daughters and their friends which I called Bukhara. Coffee spoons were thrown into my swimming pool and the girl who retrieved the most was the winner, but with no prizes.

Among my over-riding impressions of Central Asia at this time were how impoverishing Soviet agriculture had been for the environment, and how glad the Uzbeks and others were to be masters of their own destiny now and not second-class citizens in their own country, infested with Russian artisans, bureaucrats and security men. At the same time, it was evident how much the Russian emigrants loathed Gorbachev whom they held responsible for undermining their standard of living and future opportunities. Also you couldn't but be aware of the number of mosques that were springing up in every suburb and village.

BAT went ahead and built the $200 million cigarette factory in Samarkand and for a while we were the President's favourite foreign investors. So much so that when the Uzbekistan Prime Minister visited London he had been told to show his appreciation. I was invited to meet him in the Royal Garden Hotel.

The Ambassador escorted me to his suite, where the conversation was polite, and inconsequential until I brought up the question of why Uzbekistan, along with Israel and some Pacific islands, was still voting in the United Nations in support of the US's sanctions against Cuba. I had brought this up because I had recently been in Cuba and lunched with Fidel Castro who had both amused and impressed me.

The Prime Minister was surprised to hear that this was his country's position and ordered the Ambassador to make sure it was brought to his attention when he returned home. On my departure, the Ambassador accompanied me to the lift and admitted he was very embarrassed that I had brought this matter up as when he was Uzbekistan's representative at the UN, he had recommended that they adopted this position to keep in with the Americans. The next time the Cuban sanctions resolution came up at the UN, Uzbekistan voted against the US!

While I was in Prague on BAT business, I was called out of a meeting and told my sister Ann had been killed in a car crash. I was immensely fond of Ann and devastated by her loss. When she retired from Radio Free Europe - where she was dubbed by the Soviets as that 'bourgeois economist' - Ann continued to work freelance, mostly for the internationally respected think-tank, the Hudson Institute.

She also retained her flat in the German Alps as well as her house in Sheen in west London. At 63, she decided to learn to drive so that she could travel independently between Britain and Germany. Never one to go to bed early, the day she died she had risen at dawn, after having had little sleep, and set off for Germany, where she planned to work on a number of research papers at her home. It is speculated that she drove off the Autobahn to get some breakfast, fell asleep and crashed into a tree.

Ann's body was returned to London where a memorial service was held; meanwhile her colleagues in Washington held a day-long workshop in her memory. The German police efficiently collected her research documents from the scene of the accident and returned them to me.

As a leading research analyst in Central Asia for Radio Free Europe, Anne had encouraged me to develop an interest in that part of the world. When she worked in the British Consulate in Moscow in the 1950s, she had visited the Central Asian republics. Thereafter she worked for a Central Asian research bureau under a Colonel Wheeler and when that folded she was invited to join the Foreign Office Research Department.

There they told her that if she learned a Central Asian language she could receive an increase in pay. Already a linguist, reasonably fluent in French, German, Greek, Russian and Arabic, she went along with their suggestion of Uzbek but the FO could not put her in touch with an Uzbek teacher. Presumably to qualify for extra pay she would have to pass some form of exam, so she asked to see a paper or meet an examiner. They hadn't got an examiner, she was told. Could they find her an Uzbek-Russian dictionary? Eventually one was located in America and copied for her and she learned Uzbek.

Having two homes, Ann had amassed a considerable library of papers and literature on Central Asia. BAT had an ex-TASS correspondent who accompanied us around Eastern Europe and he recognised that these documents had an academic and historical interest, particularly in the former Soviet Union where censorship had been so tight. An archivist was contracted to record the material and books and, given her absorbing interest in Central Asia, it was decided to offer them to the Higher University in Tashkent. They were delighted to accept the offer and there, in a small section of their library, is where the Ann Sheehy Collection can be found today.

The last tobacco development I became involved with shortly before my retirement was Cuba. Ever since my visit there in 1957 I had taken an interest in the revolution there. During that visit I had seen a manifestation of the exploitation of the majority of the people by the few – in this case, a political clique masquerading under the banner of free market capitalism.

On my business trips to Latin America, in one country after another, I had been shocked by the affluence of the bourgeoisie and the wretchedness of the millions of poor people: the Favelas in Rio and the massive slums on the hillside as you drive into Caracas are just two glaring examples of an all-pervading social injustice.

It also disturbed me that many of these regimes where there was such poverty were supported by the US government. Fidel Castro and his small band had overthrown Batista, a client of the US. It was an amazing feat that captured the imagination of hundreds of millions throughout Latin America. I sympathised with their view.

Castro had put Cuba on the world political map. He had charisma and was recognised as a world leader of change. So that when the opportunity to invest in Cuba came after the Soviets left, I urged management to do just that. I also indicated that as the negotiations progressed I would like to meet Castro in person. In 1995, arrangements were made for a lunch at the British Embassy. Unfortunately, on the day, my driver got lost and I arrived late. Castro showed no sign of irritation and greeted me warmly. After discovering that Sheehy was an Irish name, and that I was, therefore, Celtic by descent, he insisted that we embraced as fellow Celts.

Castro's party consisted of three ministers, including his brother Raul's wife, Vilma Espin. Our party was made up of Antonio Monteiro de Castro from our Brazilian company, the British Ambassador, his commercial attaché and our Cuban contact who had arranged the meeting. Apart from Castro, Vilma Espin was the person who most impressed me. She was elegant, cultured and spoke perfect English. She had been with Castro and his guerrilla band in the mountains where she met and fell in love with Raul.

We began the meeting by talking about tobacco. Castro announced that his doctors had told him to give up smoking cigars: he now, occasionally, sucked them, he said! This led to a general discussion about health. Castro believed that there was no reason why a normal person's life span should not be 120 years. It emerged that he was an avid reader of scientific and health magazines and recently was intrigued to learn that one side of the brain was responsible for sexual activity and had asked his researchers to find out if this side could be stimulated.

We considered the US trade embargo whose effectiveness, at that time, seemed to be withering as lots of foreign investors approached the Cubans. I wondered if Castro and his regime were becoming capitalists, a proposition which he vehemently denied. We also discussed Senator Jesse Helms, one half of the Helms-Burton Act which prevented American subsidiaries doing business in Cuba. Helms, from North Carolina, was the Senate's most outspoken opponent of easing relations with Cuba. I had recently met him and found him a softly-spoken Southern Gentleman. I suggested that if Castro met Helms in private it might help improve US-Cuban relations. But he doubted it.

For our three-hour meeting, Castro was dressed in his usual Army fatigues. I mentioned that I had been surprised to see that he had attended a recent

UNESCO conference dressed in a suit with collar and tie. Castro revealed that it was the first time he had worn a tie since leaving school and had to re-learn how to do a Windsor Knot. I enquired whether he had had to wear a dinner jacket and how he had managed to tie a bow tie! He found this incredulous. Later as he left, he playfully pulled on the bow tie of an Embassy waiter only to discover that it was on elastic! "See," Castro said, "I told you so." Before departing he asked to meet the Cuban kitchen staff who were overcome with emotion at meeting their country's leader. When I left, the City Council of Havana bestowed on me a huge gold medallion as an Honorary Guest of the City.

Chapter Twenty

By the end of the Hoylake battle, I was near my retirement age of 62, but the non-executive directors wished me to stay on until I was 65 to settle the company after the traumas of Hoylake. It was agreed that I should become Non-Executive Chairman with Martin Broughton becoming Managing Director/Chief Executive. Having been hands-on for so long, I was not happy in this role and was very glad to leave at 65.

When I worked in Holland I had become exposed to the reality of the European Common Market. As an industrialist I did not get involved in the politics of the Common Agricultural Policy, but I was impressed by the Common Market's other objectives. A large market offered efficiencies of scale, better international competitors, and improved consumer offerings in products and services.

Above all, it offered the promise of an end to the kind of war that had devastated Europe for centuries. There was a stark reminder of this in my time in Amsterdam. Before the War, a significant percentage of its citizens were Jews and after 1945 this percentage was miniscule. At BAT before the War, eighty per cent of the workers in some of the factory departments were Jews. Now, there was only the factory manager. All this reflected the dreadful pogrom that the Germans inflicted on the city. Indeed, though Amsterdam suffered no bomb or battle damage, the casualty rate was among the highest of any European city.

I saw a Common Market, where national economies became interdependent, as going a long way to ridding Europe of the horrors of war. So that when I became Chairman of BAT Industries I believed it to be my mission to promote in Britain and elsewhere what eventually became the European Union.

Accordingly, I joined organisations which were active in this endeavour. The most notable were the European Round Table of Industrialists and the Action Committee for Europe. The former organisation accurately describes itself and when I joined it was a group of some ten or twelve: apart from myself, it included the Chairmen of Philips, Unilever, Fiat and Volvo. At that time our prime activity was lobbying the Prime Minister of the country next in line to chair Europe's Committee of Ministers. This was supplemented by position papers to the European Commission on matters of interest to some or all of the members. Much of it was gesturing with no follow-up.

At one of the Round Table meetings I met an Italian industrialist and his vivacious wife, both of whom I got on well with. As a result I received an invitation to join them in Venice where his company was going to be closeted in a strategy meeting with Kissinger Associates. Jill and I flew to Venice to join the party which consisted of our Italian hosts, Henry and Nancy Kissinger, Brent and Marian Scowcroft and former German Chancellor Helmut Schmidt. The Kissingers were relaxed and we chatted affably in contrast to a grim faced Schmidt who smoked incessantly and hardly said a word. Towards the end of the weekend, Kissinger remarked rather drily how was it I was going to enjoy all his words of wisdom for free. On the last night there was a presentation to Kissinger and Schmidt in St. Mark's Square. As soon as the TV floodlights came on, I saw Schmidt's face break into a rare smile, the ever consummate politician.

The Action Committee for Europe was an altogether different kettle of fish. In the UK it consisted of politicians – such as Ted Heath, Roy Jenkins and David Howell – and former civil servants, including Sir Michael Palliser, and one or two industrialists such as myself. The committee had real clout.

At this time, the major preoccupation was the single currency. There was little if any talk of a political superstructure. I recall interesting meetings with France's Jacques Delors and Germany's Helmut Kohl: I have always been a believer in a single currency. I am a firm believer that money is a store of value and this means, if anything, a rising value, such as we have recently witnessed. It alarms me that British politicians today imply that we are lucky to have a depreciating pound instead of a more stable euro.

From the start, I was for an economically integrated Europe before anyone started to build a political superstructure. Unfortunately the reverse happened and the European Parliament started writing all sorts of social law which applied to the British people without their electoral consent. I also believed that the founders of the Common Market would abide by the rules of the Single Currency and that it would bring about total economic integration. This has not happened nor is it ever likely to which has led me to change my point of view. Unless we can get a very substantial renegotiation of the treaty, I believe we should exit the EEC.

Perhaps it was because of my European credentials that I got invited to a couple of Bilderberg conferences. The Bilderberg Group – named after the Dutch hotel where they first met in 1954 and comprising leading figures in politics, business, media and academia – meets every year to discuss global issues affecting Europe and America.

It seemed to me that it was as much a social opportunity for 'yesterday's men' to renew acquaintances. At one of the meetings Garret FitzGerald, who had just lost the Irish election, was there. I chided him that he must now realise how difficult it had been for the British to govern the Irish. He agreed, but said that it was the British who had imbued in the Irish people the legacy of opposition to government.

In the early 1990s I was also invited to participate in an annual American Enterprise Institute Conference in Beaver Creek, Colorado. The cast was stellar: Presidents Ford and Giscard d'Estaing, former Prime Minister Callaghan and Chancellor Schmidt, Henry Kissinger, Brent Scowcroft and Alan Greenspan. Of the thirty delegates attending, I was the only European businessman and had been asked to give my view of the current European situation, particularly the EEC.

At one morning session I duly gave my ten minute presentation and in the coffee break I was approached by Giscard who invited Jill and myself to lunch with him and his wife. It was not a particularly appetising lunch, but Giscard was anxious to share with me his concern about the geo-political future of Europe. The Berlin Wall had come down and he was concerned that a unified Germany would dominate Europe unless there was a counterbalance which he suggested should be a revival of the Anglo-French entente. Could I do anything to promote this? I promised to think about it.

Meanwhile, Madam Giscard had been complaining about American food and particularly the coffee, which she described as eau de vaisselle (washing-up water).

That evening we were invited to a reception at President Ford's house in Beaver Creek. About an hour before we were due to set off in a fleet of limousines, the alarms rang in the rooms throughout the hotel. It was a bomb alert. We were told to leave our rooms as soon as we could and assemble on the lawns outside. Jill and I lingered somewhat to complete getting ready for the reception, but most of the American delegates rushed out in the white bathrobes provided by the hotel. President Ford sent a message saying all would be welcome at the appointed hour, however clad.

We arrived at the Ford's house at the same time as the Giscard d'Estaings. The former president greeted me and then turned to Jill, saying that he very much wanted to meet her. I said that he had met her at lunch, but he insisted and grabbed her hand and kissed her arm up to her elbow. I have never seen Jill blush with so much excitement. The following afternoon Jim Callaghan and his wife kindly invited us for tea. No kisses were exchanged.

When I got back to London, I started to consider what could be done to stimulate an Anglo-French entente. There was an Anglo-French Society, which was a somewhat moribund quango, dependent largely on the Foreign Office for funds. I had become disenchanted with organisations that depended on government funding. I recalled that the Bilderberg meeting had been a positive influence on relations with the US.

I mentioned to some of my other chairman friends, as well as to former Whitehall mandarins Michael Pallister and Lord Armstrong (who were both on our board), that I wanted to explore the idea of a Franco-British 'Mini Bilderberg' with them. They welcomed the initiative and suggested some other names, particularly Richard Lambert, Editor of the Financial Times and Nico Colchester, Deputy Editor of the Economist.

At a meeting I hosted of those interested, I suggested that the initiative should be funded privately, that is not by the Government. I also wanted it to be for today's and tomorrow's 'movers and shakers' and that it should not be a platform for 'star turns' such as heads of government or prominent visiting speakers.

These ideas were agreed and I undertook, on behalf of BAT Industries, to underwrite the cost of establishing the initiative and the first meeting. It was also agreed that there should be no more than thirty-five to forty delegates from both France and Britain and that we should select delegates from the elite civil servants, politicians, academics, media and business from the two countries. At this point, Nico Colchester and BAT's Heather Honour volunteered to progress matters and so became vital to the initiative's overall implementation. It was Nico who came up with the name: Franco-British Colloque.

It was fine having a name but we had to get French involvement in the project. Finding a prominent French industrialist or banker who would enthuse about

Franco-British relations was our first task. Members of the informal group were asked to put forward some names from which we produced a shortlist. Nico and I then flew to Paris to interview the candidates, who thought the idea had merit. But none of them were prepared to commit at this stage.

It became apparent that this was because they feared it might conflict with the Quai d'Orsay (the French Foreign Office) and even with President Pompidou. This episode demonstrated the prevalence in France of dirigisme – government intervention in economic life. We had not even consulted our own Foreign Office about the initiative, but assumed it would hear about it informally.

However, we got the go-ahead after word came from the Élysée Palace that it welcomed the initiative. From then on there was no difficulty in attracting a banker to lead the French side, nor was it difficult to attract quality delegates from among the country's elite.

The first Franco-British Colloque in December 1992, which became the model for future meetings, was held outside London – far enough away from the capital to ensure that delegates were not tempted to slip back to their office or home.

There was a very distinguished list of participants. The French side boasted the banker Gerard Worms, leading politician Jean-Pierre Chevenement and Jean-Claude Trichet, who became President of the European Central Bank. Britain fielded academics Vernon Bogdanor and Lawrence Freedman, politician Tim Renton and financier Ronald Cohen among others.

The meeting began on Thursday evening and went through to midday on Saturday. The format saw three or four issues raised on the Friday by one delegate who chaired a group of four other participants. These groups then reported back to a plenary session on the Saturday morning.

The first meeting proved a success and stimulated the French to host a second conference the following year. Ever since, they have continued as an annual event. Although to begin with, meetings were not centred on 'star turns', they eventually did with the Prince of Wales and French and British Prime Ministers inviting themselves along.

While I was involved, and in addition to those already mentioned, the following prominent figures took part in the Colloque: Alain Juppe, Louis Schweitzer, Geoff Hoon, David Howell, Peter Mandelson, Roger Lyons,

David Simon, Ian Taylor, Laurent Fabius, Elizabeth Guigou, Pascal Lamy, Dominique Strauss-Kahn, Lord Dahrendorf, Rachel Lomax, Andrew Marr, Pauline Neville-Jones, Howard Davies, Adair Turner and Philip Stephens.

Subjects discussed included political goals of Europe, economies in the European market, Franco-British relations, the future shape of the EU, unemployment in Europe, trade and international relations and privatisation and different forms of capitalism.

In the Colloque, as with Bilderberg, the elite were flattered to be invited but unlike Bilderberg, 'yesterday's' delegates are not included in 'today's' meetings. I reckon that I became a 'yesterday's' delegate in early 2000 and so resigned. I like to think that the Chevalier de la Légion D'Honneur awarded to me by President Mitterand in May 1995 was official recognition of the Colloque initiative.

Chapter Twenty-one

In 1992, when I was travelling in Canada as non-executive Chairman of BAT, I received a telephone call from Ken Clarke, the Home Secretary. He asked me to consider chairing an inquiry into the 'responsibilities and rewards' of the police in the UK. Knowing that Martin Broughton, my CEO, would be mightily relieved to see less of me, I gave a qualified 'yes' provided that I had a say in the composition of the panel. The other members of the inquiry, whom, as it turned out, I had no say in their appointment, were Sir Paul Fox, formerly head of BBC television, Professor Colin Campbell, the vice-chancellor of Nottingham University, John Bullock, a partner of the accountancy firm of Coopers Lybrand and Professor Eric Caines, the director of personnel of the NHS who had made the news by suggesting that the NHS could shed 200,000 jobs! We were given an office in Milbank and a very competent secretary in Ms Jenny Rumble.

The terms of reference of our review were to examine the rank structure, remuneration and conditions of service of the police service in the United Kingdom and to recommend what changes, if any, would be sensible to ensure that rank structures and conditions of service reflected the current roles and responsibilities of police officers; that there was enough flexibility in the distribution of rewards to ensure that responsibilities and performance were properly recognised in changing circumstances; and that remuneration was set and maintained at a level adequate to ensure the recruitment, retention and motivation of officers of the right quality.

During the inquiry we would take into account the special nature of the police officer's role, the need to ensure value for money in public spending and the principles set out in the police service statement. As well as looking at developments in pay generally, we were asked to take into account the special and different circumstances of the RUC.

This was an important inquiry of which the findings would have a lasting impact on the recruitment, man-management and operational performance of the police. As such we took it extremely seriously and approached it with an open mind.

After meeting and planning out our work, I set out on the road to visit police forces to find out what all ranks were thinking about pay and conditions. I would ask a group of constables to assemble in a room to talk about these issues after stipulating there would be no recording. That did not prevent the Police Federation, the in-house police staff association/trade union, having a pretty good idea of what was going on throughout these consultations.

On one occasion, I visited the HQ of the Kent Police and met the chief constable Paul Condon. He enthused about the mission statement he had crafted for the Kent Police and stopped a hapless constable in the corridor to declare it. The poor man had no idea. Condon later ended up in the House of Lords as 'a people's peer'.

During my travels, I went to South Armagh where I discovered to my amazement how well paid the RUC were. The poor old British squaddies were wretchedly paid in comparison. The differential was so great that I almost wondered whether the RUC had a vested interest in keeping 'the troubles' going.

In the course of the inquiry, I used to have meetings with journalists to discuss how we were approaching it and what progress we were making. One of them, Duncan Campbell of *The Guardian*, mentioned to me that his wife was the actress Julie Christie. Not being a film buff, I innocently asked him what she had appeared in. When he told me that she had just won an Oscar, I felt dreadfully embarrassed. He was charmingly unconcerned about my ignorance.

We visited over twenty forces and I was not impressed by the quasi-baronial courts I encountered when visiting Chief Constables – huge offices, large desks, a deputy this and that and a retinue of retainers. We never heard of a single instance of a sergeant visiting a constable on the beat. There was an awful lot of feather-bedding, extended sick leave before retirement and other such 'Spanish practices'. We thought the police forces needed incentivising by annually polling the local community to whom they were answerable rather than being judged by easily manipulated crime statistics. This did not go down well. Finally we presented our report in July 1993.

We must have done something right for the Police Federation, which had been suspicious of and resistant to the inquiry from day one, took it on themselves to produce mugs and badges saying 'No to Sheehy'. Expressing 'shock and dismay' in the July edition of the magazine *Police*, which incidentally had my face splashed across the front cover, the Federation described the report as 'a blueprint for disaster' and called a huge protest rally at Wembley which was attended by over 23,000 off-duty police officers.

Roger Gale who was the MP for Thanet North approached me to arrange a meeting with the police in his and neighbouring constituencies. A venue was agreed at Margate on the Friday evening of the August Bank Holiday with my proviso that no press were to be admitted to the actual proceedings. I was then informed that the meeting was off because all police leave had been cancelled due to a Mods and Rockers rally on the same date. On Saturday a police inspector visited Roger during his surgery. Roger remarked that the Mods and Rockers demonstration appeared to have passed off quietly. "What demonstration?" enquired the inspector. The Police Federation had stitched us up!

Back at BAT, once the report had been published, I was approached by Alan Eastwood, the former national chairman of the Police Federation looking for a job. So I gave him lunch and asked him why, within half an hour of the report being published, it had been rubbished by the Federation who accused us of kicking it 'in the vital parts'. He told me that there was a bit in the back about reforming it and that "we could not publicly get away with just highlighting this single recommendation we disagreed with, so we had to rubbish it all". This surprised me for all I could recall was recommending that 'matters concerning the management of the Police Federation should be left to the Police Federation. We see no reason for such matters to be dealt with in the National Code'!

Meanwhile Ken Clarke, who had become Chancellor of the Exchequer, had been replaced by Michael Howard. *The Guardian*'s leading article on 1 July called the report radical and while in no doubt that Clarke would have 'pushed through the package', it correctly wondered 'whether Howard had the chutzpah to do so'. By the beginning of October, under pressure from Tory MPs in marginal constituencies who were at the receiving end of Police Federation lobbying, it looked as if Howard had more or less washed his hands of our report.

In a *Daily Telegraph* article entitled *Law and Disorder*, I wrote that the goal of chief police officers and of our report was the same as that set by Sir Robert Peel, a founding father of the Conservative Party and inventor of the modern police service 170 years ago. "I wish to obtain", he said, "as perfect a system of police as is consistent with the character of a free country". I went on to urge the Home Secretary as his successor 'to realise that aim for our own times'.

At the end of October, Howard finally ruled in favour of some of the less contentious recommendations, a compromise summarised by *The Financial Times* as 'given the skilled campaigning of the well-organized police staff associations' and 'with the government lacking confidence in its ability to carry a parliamentary majority, it is perhaps the best that could have been achieved'. It was an intensely disappointing result but over time, I'm glad to say that many of our 270 or so recommendations have since been implemented.

Chapter Twenty-two

At BAT Industries we encouraged our subsidiaries to become involved in their local communities. Although the company itself only employed 100 or so people at its Head Office in Victoria Street, London, we became involved in social initiatives across the capital.

There had been riots in Brixton in 1981 with unemployment – mainly among black youths – the root cause. The area was crumbling with little investment in buildings and a high crime rate. We leased a former department store in the high street and converted it into a centre for small businesses. It was particularly aimed at encouraging entrepreneurs from the ethnic minority groups.

Although we offered business advice to prospective entrepreneurs, the Brixton centre never succeeded in attracting enough tenants. Those who did rent office space were established businesses seeking low-cost secure premises. Elsewhere, two similar centres were sponsored by our factories in Southampton and Liverpool.

I joined the Prince's Trust when it started in 1976 but when its directors began to stage manage all the meetings I became disillusioned and withdrew. The Prince of Wales later gripped the organisation and turned it into a successful small business initiative.

Norman Fowler and his Ministry introduced a scheme whereby Captains of Industry were encouraged to involve themselves in small enterprises which would then have access to low-price Government finance. But the final say-so was with junior bureaucrats who did not understand risk. As a result, this scheme withered.

All in all, there was a lot of endeavour in terms of our community involvement but with little to show for it. So, when Kenneth Baker announced his proposal for setting up City Technology Colleges (CTCs) in deprived areas to be partly, but significantly, funded by companies who would run them in conjunction with the Department of Education and Science (but with local authorities having no say), it appeared to me that BAT should get involved. Fortunately, the board was very supportive and among my colleagues, Gerald Dennis, was particularly enthusiastic and volunteered to progress its implementation.

Although school initiatives in urban areas have become more closely identified with new Labour's education policy from 1997, CTCs were a Tory idea as far back as 1986. CTCs are state-backed, yet independent, schools set up in deprived urban areas catering for up to 1,000 students aged from 11 to 18 and with all abilities and from all backgrounds.

The CTC programme was a ground-breaking scheme designed to offer a general education, but unique in that it equipped students with scientific, technological and practical skills. This was what appealed to BAT and encouraged us to get involved. We could also see that CTCs offered wider parental choice, while its vocational bias would provide a strong skills base for the local community and would create a focus for a dialogue between industrialists and educationalists.

BAT decided to take up the Government's invitation for businesses to commit cash, equipment and general support to the CTCs. As a responsible employer, we had long been concerned about the effects of sustained and high unemployment on people and businesses in affected communities. In addition, we were also concerned about the lack of technical skills among school leavers – a shortage we felt that could become acute.

CTCs seemed to help answer some of these needs. They would prepare youngsters for the world of work and go a long way towards providing them with the necessary training and background for a career in business. CTCs also provided synchronicity: they complemented a programme we were already involved with which looked to create jobs in area of high unemployment.

Having decided to get involved, it was then a question of where. We were urged to establish a CTC in Portsmouth, but this did not seem to me to be a deprived area. I insisted that we establish our CTC where it would make a difference. Liverpool, where we had a factory, was approached, but surprisingly, the Anglican Bishop David Sheppard and Catholic Archbishop Derek Worlock were opposed to it, as was the local educational establishment. The offer of a CTC had not been supported by the Labour Party and was an anathema to local councils and the National Union of Teachers.

Any CTC needed a site within the catchment area of the students being targeted. Local authorities which controlled urban planning could, and did, put in place many obstacles. We turned our attention to the North-East and a property was eventually located in Middlesbrough on Teesside, the site of a former Catholic school which had closed. As a result, we did not need planning permission to re-open it as a new school.

Thus, we became a major sponsor of the Teesside Technology College putting in one million pounds along with contributions from British Steel, the Davy Corporation and Cameron Hall Developments (whose founder Sir John Hall later became chairman of Newcastle United), making the total contribution £1.6 million. These organisations formed the school's Trust body.

The next important step was to appoint a head. The school's first Principal, John Paddick, was enthusiastic about CTCs and became the scheme's local champion. He worked tirelessly and with immense competence to establish and run the school, which opened as Macmillan College in September 1989, the second CTC to be launched nationally. He had a very good reputation and was able to persuade dedicated teachers that a CTC was going to deliver a different and worthwhile education, free from political meddling. Teachers in a CTC work longer hours than their local authority counterparts for the same pay.

The CTC needed students and the plan was to recruit them from local primaries, each year adding another layer until after five years it would be covering a range from 11 to 16. The requirement was that the students had to come from a cross-section of abilities in the catchment area.

John Paddick approached the Education Authority to ask them to provide candidates and they refused. He then took to the streets and knocked on doors. It was not easy to persuade parents, many of them poorly educated and single mothers, that this new school would be different and better. Many had been the target of other Government initiatives and had concluded that these did not improve their lot. Paddick was operating in an area where youth unemployment was nearly twenty per cent and school absenteeism over thirty per cent. While he wanted students, he also needed a parent who would support the child at school and with their homework.

Paddick was responsible for Macmillan's day-to-day running under supervision of the Board of Governors. While adhering to the National Curriculum, the school focused on giving its students an awareness of the world of industry and commerce, using modern technology and involving businesses and parents.

Macmillan was launched amid great enthusiasm and optimism locally and after the first year the school was an amazing success: absenteeism was under five per cent and in the second year primary school entry was over-subscribed by more than 100%. One problem that arose and persisted for some years was a lack of outdoor sports facilities. Although there were local authority-owned playing fields adjacent to Macmillan, which were not used on weekdays, the council refused permission for the school to use them. Fortunately, John Hall – who was one of the Patrons – had an extensive estate and made land available for the school's sports needs with students bussed there and back.

The local authority's attitude to the playing fields was typical of its hostility and its dedicated enmity was disgraceful. Macmillan had a difficult relationship with the local Cleveland Education Authority. Quite simply, its senior officers and committee members – being Labour – were openly hostile to the whole idea of CTCs. In the face of this hostility, the school's Chairman of Governors sought advice from the DES.

Another concern within BAT at this time was the Government's overall commitment to the CTC programme. Our initial involvement was for seven years and we were prepared to increase this to a rolling seven-year support, but we wanted to know where the Government stood.

The Department of Education and Science appeared to be reconsidering its decision to establish CTCs in Derbyshire, Wandsworth and Telford. So we wrote to Angela Rumbold, a Minister at the DES, detailing our concerns about the Government's commitment to expenditure levels.

BAT reflected its level of commitment by organising industrial experience for six of Macmillan's senior staff, which saw John Paddick, a fluent Spanish speaker, working for a week with our company in Venezuela. Meanwhile, the school went from strength to strength. Governors' Reports from 1990 to 1992 showed the progress being made: student numbers rose from 352 to 552 – with a short-term target of 950 – the curriculum was developing, along with growing levels of performance inside and outside the classroom.

One interesting technique adopted by Paddick was to encourage single parents to join their children in class so that they could help them. In essence, it was a vicarious form of adult education. But it worked in getting both to become more engaged.

As a mark of its progress, Macmillan enjoyed a visit from the Education Secretary, Ken Clarke, which helped place it firmly on the map as a centre of excellence employing technology and science and embracing the business ethic. This was followed by a visit by Gillian Shephard when she took over at the DES in 1994.

In the summer of 1994 John Paddick retired and was succeeded by Bob Howarth. John went on to advise BAT on its educational projects and become an Ofsted Inspector. At this time, I had the pleasure of opening a Technology Wing at the school. A year later, further progress came with proposals for a new Sixth Form Centre at a projected cost of £2.2 million: £500,000 was being sought from BAT, which we were enthusiastic to provide, matched by similar funding from the DES.

We had chosen to sponsor a CTC on Teesside because of its high youth unemployment and being an area with a desperate need for new technology and new industry. It seemed to us that an education that could equip young people with the right skills must help bring business back to Middlesbrough.

By the time I retired, Macmillan was firmly established, though a significant problem was emerging as Asian shopkeepers deliberately moved into the catchment area so that their numerous children could attend the school. As a result, Macmillan had a higher percentage of Asian students than of Asians in the catchment area. The intention was to help the long-term unemployed and underclass families that lived there.

It was hoped that Macmillan would act as a competitive spur to the Cleveland Education Authority to improve the performance of its schools. But, alas, officials only whinged that they could not compete with a school endowed with greater resources. It was the usual excuse of the Left that it was unfair. Unfortunately, their concept of fairness means levelling down instead of rising up. It was also hoped that Macmillan would, and indeed did, develop a pool of youngsters with relevant skills for industry and business and that they would attract investment back to the area. Unfortunately, many of the former students then took their skills elsewhere – mainly to the South.

Inside six years, Macmillan had become one of the most rewarding community projects BAT had undertaken. Indeed, it was to be our flagship project. The school continues to flourish today as Macmillan Academy with 1,500 students drawn from across the Middlesbrough area.

Meanwhile, in Sandwich – where Jill and I have a cottage – there was a secondary school that I became aware of that was limping along and bordering on failure. When I told Lady Julia Pender, who was a school governor and a friend, of my enthusiasm for CTCs, she informed me that the new head of the school was interested in the concept. A visit to the Macmillan College was organised and BAT Industries staff helped them to become a CTC. Today, Sandwich Technology School is flourishing and has been successful expanded and is over-subscribed.

In the early 1990s some newspaper articles appeared stating that the Royal Commonwealth Society (RCS) had a debt crisis and was considering selling its library of books and memorabilia, mostly photographs. It was speculated that it would either be sold piecemeal or to an American university.

Both possibilities seemed undesirable to me. My Commonwealth credentials are extensive. My father was in the ICS; I was born in Burma when it was part of the Empire; I was educated in England and Australia; I'd been stationed in the Gold Coast, Nigeria, Jamaica and Barbados and visited, with BAT, most of the Commonwealth countries. I also have a modest library, many of whose books are about the history of the Empire and the Commonwealth.

The thought of what was described as a 'unique collection' being broken up and going abroad appalled and worried me. I let it be known that if there was an appeal to save the library, I would be happy to join the committee. The reply came back that there was no committee, but that if I would chair such an appeal the RCS would give me every encouragement. So, I did.

Fortunately, two immensely generous benefactors, Sir Peter Moores and Garfield Weston, had already been in touch with the RCS and indicated that they would support any appeal. So I invited them to join the committee.

Before we could really seek funds, we had to establish what price the RCS put on the library. The committee did not want to pay for an expensive valuation when, in fact, all the RCS wanted was three million pounds, which was its debt to NatWest. The second issue we had to resolve was where would the library be located? Neither the RCS nor the committee wanted it to be a 'static' collection in a solo site; rather, we wanted it to be part of a 'living' library, preferably one of record.

We also wanted it to be located in or near London, so there were really only three candidates: the Bodleian Library, Oxford and the libraries at London and Cambridge universities. We received a message from Buckingham Palace, however, that the Queen hoped the RCS library could remain in London –

possibly at Canary Wharf which, at that time, was in trouble and had a lot of empty office space.

In the event, only Cambridge University had the capacity to house the library and was willing to pay for its cataloguing and transfer from London. Cambridge also agreed that a Commonwealth Reading Room would be part of the next university library expansion.

The project got off to a flying start with a generous donation from the Queen and £500,000 each from Sir Peter Moores and Garfield Weston, who actually asked me whether his sum was enough! There was a disappointing response from multi-national companies which had interests in the Commonwealth, and particularly from NatWest. The bank declined to donate even though it had been enjoying a generous rate of interest on its loan to the RCS.

There was an amusing incident when we were invited to visit an MP in his office at the House of Commons. He thought he could prise some money out of one of the Foreign & Commonwealth Office budgets. But just after the meeting began, he apologised in advance that we would most likely be interrupted as No.10 had rung to say that the Israeli Prime Minister was making an unplanned visit and therefore the scheduled delivery of prize-winning pork sausages from a Midlands butcher, who was one of his constituents, needed to be delayed. Consequently the butcher was waiting in a lay-by waiting for the green light from the MP who in turn was waiting for the all-clear from Downing Street. We later left with no more bulletins on the sausages or the money for the appeal but we had had an amusing morning.

The appeal eventually raised £3.5 million and the library, which also contained some 250,000 photographs – many from the Royal Collection – is now part of the Cambridge University Library. The committee initially decided that the surplus £500,000 should be used to add books, but this was not actively pursued by the Cambridge Librarian who thought that the photographic collection was of greater value to students and researchers by being catalogued and available on the Internet. This, however, would cost £750,000.

It was also decided that there should be a dedicated computer link between the RCS in London and the Cambridge University Library. The surplus, plus interest, had eventually grown into around £750,000, and it was agreed to spend this sum on both photographic and computer link projects. One

Cambridge librarian later estimated the value of the RCS collection at £12 million, the most valuable collection of its kind that the university had ever received.

In honour of my retirement, in 1996 the company decided to establish a £1.5 million Sir Patrick Sheehy Chair for a Professorship of International Relations at the Centre of International Studies at Cambridge University. It aroused a certain amount of controversy; egged on by the British Medical Journal who found it 'hard to make a moral distinction between the tobacco industry and the drug cartels', a vociferous group of dons campaigned to turn it down on the grounds that was funded by a tobacco company. This was somewhat ironic as the Chairman of the Cambridge University Appeal in the USA at the time was the Chairman of Philip Morris Inc. In the event it was put to the vote of all 3,500 dons and was passed overwhelmingly.

About this time an appeal was launched for an Oxford American Library which would be an integral part of the Bodleian and I was invited to join the appeal committee. Brown & Williamson in America had recently bought a low-priced brand from an entrepreneur who cherished his links with England. He was persuaded to give $500,000 to the appeal. A room in the library would bear his family name and the Cecil Rhodes Foundation would match his donation.

Generously endowed by the Harmsworth family, it was eventually named the Vere Harmsworth Library and it was opened by President Clinton in a ceremony I attended. Located in the Rothermere American Institute, it is Oxford's main research library for US Studies.

On my retirement from BAT in 1995, Ken Clarke, then the Chancellor of the Exchequer, allowed me to have a cocktail party in No.11. This attracted unfair criticism from the Daily Telegraph. I had been to a party there before when John Major was Chancellor in 1989. I was met by Subba Row, the cricketer, who told me that Sir Len Hutton wanted to talk to me. As I am no cricketer or indeed fan of the game, I was mildly surprised and when we eventually met up all he wanted was 'inside information' about BAT. He was most affable and sadly died the next year.

Chapter Twenty-three

Just before I retired, I was called by the Canadian entrepreneur Fergus McCann who had just bought Celtic FC for £9.5 million. I thought he wanted BAT sponsorship but what he really had in mind was my services as a director. Not being a football fan, I told him that it wasn't up my street. "Football fans? I've got 40,000 of them! What I need is someone with business talents." After a certain amount of to-ing and fro-ing, I agreed and became a non-director in March 1996, a role that was to last for the next twelve years. Two memorable incidents come to mind.

McCann had bought a talented Dutch striker, Pierre Van Hooijdonk, from a Dutch team for a good price. He soon became a prolific goal scorer for Celtic and demanded a pay rise as other more recently purchased players were paid more than him. He and McCann were unable to agree terms and he was eventually sold to an English league club with a rider that if he scored twenty or more goals for them before a certain date, Celtic would be entitled to another £500,000. Come the last game in January, the cut-off date, when Van Hooijdonk had scored nineteen goals, his team were awarded a penalty. He took it, scored and Celtic were half a million pounds richer! I have always wondered what the directors of that club have thought about the manager's decision to allow Van Hooijdonk to take the penalty.

At one particularly noisy AGM at Celtic FC's ground, attended by over 6,000 shareholders, there was widespread unhappiness about the team's performance. One shareholder asked whether the board intended to strengthen the team and the manager replied that he was in the process of doing just that but it involved assessing talented individuals by personally watching them play. This was too much for another shareholder who jumped to his feet and pointing his finger at the board exclaimed: "You lot couldn't spot the Pope if he was in the directors' box at Ibrox Park!"

Algy Cluff invited me to join the board of Cluff Mining as a non-executive director which I did for a few years. At this stage he also owned *The Spectator Magazine* which he had bought from Henry Keswick and he asked me, Sir Owen Green and Ludovic Kennedy to join the board. At the time the company was making substantial losses although Algy had replaced the editor Alexander Chancellor with Charles Moore and circulation had begun to rise. Algy then sold it to the Australian Fairfax publishing group who in turn sold it to Conrad Black who had a controlling interest in the *Telegraph* group. Subsequently Conrad appointed Norman Tebbit to the board which caused Ludovic to resign, saying that he could not sit at the same table as a man who wanted to abolish the BBC. During my tenure as a non-exec, Charles Moore was followed by Dominic Lawson, Frank Johnson, Boris Johnson and Matthew d'Ancona. In late 2004, the Barclay brothers, who had acquired the magazine when they bought the *Telegraph* group from Black, appointed Andrew Neill as editor-in-chief. Soon after he unceremoniously kicked us off the board and our complimentary copies ceased abruptly.

The attraction of *The Spectator* board was not so much the meetings but the dinners afterwards with contributors and journalists. At one of these dinners I met the Home Secretary David Blunkett who had been invited by the publisher, a young American woman called Kimberley Fortier. Their affair at this stage had not yet become public. I was surprised by how amiable Blunkett and Tebbit were in conversation.

Algy also approached me to be the Chairman of Ashanti Gold and as I had fond memories of working in Ghana as a young man and later as a director of BAT, I said I would be interested. Behind the scenes, President Rawlings had told Algy that he thought the board had been acting too much in its own interests. I had dinner with Sam Jonah, the CEO, in London who was reserved but very cordial and he invited me to attend the Annual General Meeting shortly to be held in Obuasi. When I arrived, I was appalled by what a slum the town had become since I was last there but at least the mine where the meeting took place appeared well maintained.

It was clear to me that the board did not want me. Among the directors was Lynda Chalker with whom I had a frosty conversation during lunch. She had annoyed me when as Minister for Europe she had accepted BAT's hospitality at Wimbledon and almost immediately afterwards taken a strong anti-tobacco stance. There was no point in staying on so I returned to London.

Sometime later I was invited by the government to meet President Rawlinson to talk about the chairmanship. Put up at a top hotel, I waited and waited. Eventually about three hours before my flight was due to leave for

London, I was summoned in the dark to a house surrounded by a high wall and ushered into rather gloomy living room when I was met by the President's wife Nana Konadu, a petite and very bright young lady. After a short time we were joined by President Rawlinson who was in the last month of his term in office. While he expressed his pleasure at my willingness to take on the challenging task of chairing Ashanti, he was more inclined to talk about whether he would be prosecuted after he stood down for the deaths of six generals at the time of his 1979 coup. I could only listen. Fortunately, with his help, I managed to catch my plane.

Campbell Fraser, who was on the board of BAT, put my name forward to BP as a non-executive director and I joined it in 1984 when the government still had a stake in it and was represented on the board by Tony Barber and Tom Jackson, the General Secretary of the Post Office Workers Union. At first the board used to meet every two weeks although I can't remember discussing anything of great importance until the decision was made to sell the government's holding. The board was said to be unanimous about this but I was certainly not consulted! Not that I would have objected. During the run up to the sale, the market collapsed and the underwriters squealed for a postponement. Nigel Lawson as Chancellor of the Exchequer would not entertain the idea as he considered that they had all done very well out of previous government privatisations.

Part of our duties was to visit BP installations and the first place I went to was the headquarters of their North Sea operations in Aberdeen, headed by John Browne who was not a board director at the time. He was most impressive as a manager. I also visited Alaska and Columbia, the latter had Tony Hayward in charge. A very quietly spoken and youngish-looking man, he clearly enjoyed the respect of his colleagues. After Sir Peter Walters stood down as chairman in 1992, there was considerable discussion about who should be the next chairman and CEO: it boiled down to either Rodney Chase or Bob Horton. Chase really decided it by saying he would not stand in Horton's way. There was no doubt that Horton was very competent, particularly in the area of financial management, including M&A.

However, none of us at the time spotted his 'folie de grandeur'. For instance, he immediately ordered four Gulfstream executive jets for each of the heads of operations although none of them had actually requested one. He became more and more grand and distanced from his colleagues to such an extent that they were grumbling to the board about him although not to me. By June 1992, these board members thought it was so serious that a meeting was warranted. I agreed to a meeting in BAT's flat in Victoria Street at which it was decided that Horton must go and I suggested that we should appoint a non-executive chairman and a CEO. These roles were subsequently filled by Lord Ashburton of Barings Bank and David Simon, the COO. Although John Browne had been a great protégé of Horton, as far as I know he raised no objection. After Ashburton, in 1995 we had Sir Peter Sutherland, a highly capable Irish lawyer, as chairman but he failed to keep John Browne under control and the two were at loggerheads. He left the board in 1995 and I finally stood down in 1998 after fourteen years. My abiding memory was how extraordinarily bad BP was at forecasting the oil price which meant that it was equally bad at assessing the viability of major capital projects. But I guess that is the same for all oil companies and other commodity dependent organizations.

When I had been in Cuba and met with Fidel Castro, a company called Sherritt International Corporation was just starting up its business there. Sherritt Gordon had been a small mining company with a refinery at Fort Saskatchewan in Alberta, Canada with a patent for extracting nickel and cobalt from lateritic ore by a high pressure acid-leeching process. Fast running out of source material at home, the company was taken over after a bitter proxy fight in 1990 by the financier Ian Delaney who immediately set about reorganizing it and by 1994 it was generating an $80-million profit on sales of $921 million, which included the revenues of a Joint Venture with the Cuban Moa nickel and cobalt mine.

The year after I joined the board in 1995, the Cuban air force shot down two Florida-based aircraft belonging to the Brothers to the Rescue anti-Castro exile group, which had been formed to aid Cuban refugees trying to flee the island. This explosive incident focused US attention on Cuba and resulted in Congress passing the hardline anti-Castro Helms-Burton Act in March 1996. As it was seen as exploiting assets in Cuba, Sherritt fell foul of the Act and its directors, now classified as 'traffickers in banned goods', barred from travel to the US. So together with my wife and children [until they were 18] I was banned from entering the USA for 12 years. Another UK director, Rupert Pennant-Rea, also found himself in the frame but eventually resigned when he took on the chairmanship of *The Economist* whose readership was mostly in the US.

To legislate in haste is rarely the right thing to do and as far as I can tell, the Helms-Burton Act has cost the US billions of dollars in lost trade, failed to stem foreign investment into Cuba and made no impact on the political fortunes of Fidel and Raoul Castro.

Despite this upset, Sherritt became the first foreign capitalist company to hold a board meeting in Cuba since Castro's revolution in 1959. We continued to have an annual board meeting in Cuba and helped develop a golf course at Varadero on the old Dupont estate. The company went on to own oil and gas operations in Cuba as well as a stake in the Energas power utility [1998], which had plants powered by Sherritt from previously flared gas. For a while we were the darlings of the Cuban government and Sherritt was very close to Fidel Castro who would come to the reception after our Golf Tournament.

After acquiring Dynatec Mining in 2007, the company became inveigled in the Ambatovy nickel and cobalt project in Madagascar. The ore was 150 kilometres away from the coast where the refinery was to be built at Toamasima and the ore was to be slurried down a pipeline to the plant. The original cost was estimated at around $3.4 billion but the final cost including financing came out at $6.5 billion and was therefore unlikely to generate any free cash flow for a considerable time. I visited Madagacar on two or three occasions. It is a wretchedly poor country but surprisingly the inhabitants are mostly of Indonesian origin, not African. They even speak a version of Indonesian.

For about four years I was a director of John Latsis's private bank, EFG. Board meetings were in London and Zurich. Among the other directors was William Rees-Mogg, former editor of *The Times*. I can't recall him ever saying anything at board meetings but he was a delightful and interesting conversationalist at lunch time. After the collapse of the banking system, regulation and compliance became the order of the day. Monitoring the complex financial products that were so fashionable at the time was beyond me and I resigned.

Another job I took on was Chairman of a smoked salmon business in the Scottish Borders. The business was owned by a friend of mine, Albert Abela, who ran a large international catering and hotel operation. It was really a cottage establishment which needed modernising in order to meet the exacting standards of major supermarket chains. With strong price competition from Norway, it was barely profitable. Albert suddenly died in 2002 and his estate drastically attacked the cost base and I was fired.

Asda Property, a private property company run by Manny Davidson, invited me on its board. Another non-executive was a Chartered Accountant. Between us we helped Manny present his company in a way more acceptable to other investors. He decided to merge the company with British Land in 2001, so there was no place for us non-executive directors. In 2006, British Land bought out Manny's remaining 50% stake for £253 million.

In 1996, my son-in-law, Hadyn Cunningham of Merrill Lynch, suggested my name to Sir Martyn Arbib as Chairman of Perpetual Income and Growth Investment Trust [PIGIT] which had just been launched. This was a lively convivial board which met in an old rectory by the Thames at Henley. During my tenure I persuaded the board in 2005 to launch a hostile bid for an investment trust, Securities Trust of Scotland. It failed but the publicity surrounding the bid did bring our company's performance to the attention of a wider audience of investors and the share price responded positively. I resigned when I was 70; those were the days before ageism!

After the coalition government come to power in the 2010 General Election and taking his cue from David Cameron's speech about the Big Society, Charlie Elphicke, the new MP for Dover, came up with a scheme to stop the privatisation of the Port of Dover and the Dover Harbour Board [DHB], which the Labour Government had tabled in its dying days. By forming a charitable trust run by Dover citizens to take it over, the profits from the Port of Dover could be used for the development of the town. On the other hand, the objective of the management of DHB, which ran the port, was to privatise it whereby they would all be handsomely rewarded by a foreign investor.

Dover indeed is a sad run down town and the DHB has never been an active partner in its development. It had little industry but a lot of through traffic. As a major entry point to the UK it was a shabby sight. The Big Society was said to offer the opportunity for local people to manage activities in their area.

Charlie formed a Trust – the Dover People's Port Trust –with a board of local businessmen. Through his old City contacts, he enticed a merchant banker, lawyers and a PR company to join the endeavour on a no-win no-fee basis. They proposed that the board should be strengthened by some 'heavyweight' names and Algy Cluff and I, who both lived nearby, were happy to join.

On 1 November, we duly presented our offer to Downing Street for buying the port under the auspices of the Big Society.

We invited citizens of Dover District Council to become members of the Trust at £10 each and enlisted some 1,100. A referendum was held in March 2011 when a higher turnout than at local elections was achieved with over 97% voting for the resolution: "Do you oppose the private sale of the Port of Dover as proposed by the DHB and support its transfer to the community of Dover instead?"

Vera Lynn graciously came to a public meeting on the beach when we were campaigning for support. I had the pleasure of sitting beside her and was surprised when she told me that her signature song 'The White Cliffs of Dover' was written by an American!

After that, negotiations started with civil servants of the Department of Transport [Ports]. It was evident that the transfer of ownership of the Port of Dover to the citizens of Dover would lead to a rash of other ports demanding the same opportunity. There would be no need for a Ports Ministry!

In December 2012, Charlie Elphicke achieved his objective – the Government ruled against privatisation and he later kept his seat in the 2015 election with an increased lead over Labour.

After five years and five Ministers nothing has happened as far as The Big Society and the Port of Dover are concerned. Another case of Government being all talk and no action.

Over the years, I have come to the conclusion that the contribution of non-executive directors to the running of boards is over-rated and in fact can be disastrous as witnessed by the collapse of the banking system in Britain.

Some boards end up with only one executive director which virtually allows him or her to set the agenda and decide what information the board should or should not have. Few of the non-executive directors have any experience of the business they are in, even as customers. I also think the fees that non-executive chairmen are paid are quite ridiculous - £500,000 to £750,000 a year for a Footsie 100 company - are ludicrous when there are only six meetings a year.

Many of the appointments have attracted civil servants whose public sector pensions are lower than their board fees. Apart from leaving early to take up these lucrative appointments and the ensuing loss to government departments of senior talent, the money means so much to them that I question whether any of them are prepared to say no to a forceful CEO and tender their resignation.

Finally, I am of the opinion that the whole movement to non-executive directors has been a cop out by the investment companies and a huge opportunity for head-hunters, some of whom only search for non-executives! There has been no measurable improvement in the economic performance of British companies since the advent of non-executives nor any demonstrable benefit to shareholders as far as I can see.

The world today is a very different place to the one I was born into eighty or so years ago. Much of my early life was lived in the twilight days of a Far East empire and then in the shadow of world war. Separation from one's parents for long periods of time was not unusual and I knew nothing else. My children and grandchildren fortunately have not had to experience the same uncertainty and insecurity but, at the same time, I attribute much of my success to my ability to stand my ground learnt in this formative period of my life. Self-reliance, resilience and independence of mind, however painfully acquired, stand one in good stead in the competitive world of business.

Is there a secret to a successful career in business? First I always count my blessings, namely that I was born with a strong constitution and imbued with a large dollop of common sense from an early age. Impatience, often seen as a negative characteristic, has for me been a strength. I hate complacency and smugness because the very essence of commerce and industry and indeed politics, science and the arts is about anticipating and managing change. The tobacco business is in many ways a bellwether for change. It was a pioneer of process engineering [the quantum jump from hand-rolled to machine-made cigarettes], of brands and marketing, and, to survive, it has had to be responsive to consumer preferences, social strictures and shareholder needs. During my time with BAT, the company underwent a number of dramatic transformations in order to not only survive but to emerge stronger and more robust. I was lucky enough to have been in the thick of it, on the cusp of change in post-colonial Africa and the Far East and when new markets suddenly opened up after the fall of the Berlin Wall.

For me, business has been an intoxicating elixir of people, places and products. In BAT our stakeholders covered an enormous array of interests, from growers to consumers, from governments to supranational institutions, from shop floor employees to senior managers, from retail concessionaires to remote village shops. Above all, I always believed in making the right decisions for our shareholders and I am immensely proud that BAT has never failed to pay a dividend since its first year of trading. It may be an old fashioned view but shareholders, be they institutions or private individuals, part with their money to a company's board of directors in return for a reward, an act based on trust. Under my stewardship, it was an honour to continue this tradition and to preside over a gratifying increase in market capitalisation of the company.

Having fun as well as working hard is all important. I thoroughly enjoyed my golfing days – always a good excuse to combine business with pleasure – and all the initiatives I took with BAT's support for the arts and the wider community.